THE AUTHORITY OF THE BELIEVER

How To Take Dominion in Every Area of Your Life!

KENNETH W. GILMORE, SR.

The Authority of the Believer

Printed in the United States of America
International Standard Book Number: 09748944-5-1

Unless otherwise noted, all Scripture quotations are from the New King James Version.

Produced by Gilmore Publishing.

DEDICATION

This Book is dedicated to my good friend, Andrew Atkinson, who has been a faithful friend and colleague in the ministry. We are truly soul mates. May God continue to bless your life and your ministry.

ACKNOWLEDGEMENTS

I have learned over the years to be successful in anything you need the support and encouragement of others. This book would not have come to fruition without the editorial assistance of my editor, Diane Fischler, and production artist, Cathleen Kwas, who always gives my manuscript that professional touch. Thanks you so much for professional expertise.

PREFACE

You

(Name)

As a believer, you do not have to live a defeated, disappointed and depressed life. You can learn to take dominion in every area of your life, and exercise the authority you have as a child of God!

TABLE OF CONTENTS

Chapter One

THE SPIRIT OF THE ANTI-CHRIST

BELOVED BELIEVE NOT EVERY SPIRIT, BUT TEST THE SPIRITS to see whether they are of God for many false prophets have gone out into the world. Hereby we know the Spirit of God, every spirit that confesses that Jesus Christ has come in the flesh is of God, every spirit that confesses not that Jesus Christ has come in the flesh is not of God, this is the spirit of the Anti-Christ, which you have heard was coming, and is even now already in the world. You are of God, little children, and have over come them, because greater is He that is in you than he who is in the world. They are of the world, and they speak of the world and the world hears them, but we are of God, and he that knows God hears us. He that is not of God hears us; hereby we know the spirit of truth and the spirit of error" (1 John 4:1-6).

THE UNSEEN WORLD

We are so often moved and motivated by what we experience through our physical senses in the "natural world."

In this passage of Scripture, John contrasts the Spirit of truth and the spirit of error. This teaches believers that behind the physical or the natural world of our senses (seeing, tasting, touching, smelling, hearing) there is a real and unseen world. We are so often moved and motivated by what we experience through our physical senses in the "natural world."

Many believers operate off their sensory mechanism rather than on their faith, which means they cannot really serve God because they allow their senses to dictate how they will act. When Sunday comes, and they feel some sort of pain, their physical senses say to their brain they should not go to church.

When clouds appear in the sky and it looks like it is

going to rain, they will say, "Well, I don't want go to church because it is going to rain." In other words, they are controlled by what they see and how they feel. Believers should not operate on the basis of what is visible when it comes to biblical teaching or spiritual matters. In 2 Corinthians 5:7, Paul says: "We walk by faith and not by sight." Paul, again in Romans 10; 17, says that "faith comes by hearing and hearing by the Word of God."

Lining up your life with the Word of God releases your faith to do what the Word of God says you need to do. Do not be persuaded by your senses to do that which is contrary to the Word of God. The unbeliever lives by the philosophy: "I don't believe unless I see." In John 20:19, Jesus said to Thomas: "Blessed are those who believe and yet they do not see."

Lining up your life with the Word of God releases your faith to do what the Word of God says you need to do.

In other words, the believer does not direct his life based on his desires of living in the natural world—but by the Spirit of God. Hebrews 11:1 says: "Faith is the substance of things hoped for and the evidence of things not seen." The believer does not depend upon the aid of his five senses.

In Genesis 12, God told Abraham to pack up everything he had and leave his relatives and his home and go to a new land. God had not yet revealed to him where He wanted Abraham to go, yet Abraham did what God told him to do. God instructed Abraham and Sarah they were going to have a son. Abraham was 100 years old and Sarah 90 years of age. Both of them were way past the child-producing and child-bearing years. This was impossible, yet God was going to do something that was beyond their physical limitations based on their faith in Him. God sometimes asks His people to do things that defy logic—and this is what faith is all about. In Genesis 22, God told Abraham to offer up his only son Isaac. Isaac represented Abraham's future. God said to Abraham, offer him up. Abraham went up to Mount Moriah to offer up his only son. God tested Abraham to see where his faith was. God asked him to do the absurd.

God instructed Israel to cross the Red Sea. This was impossible! Yet under the leadership of Moses they went forward trusting in God. On one occasion Jesus sent His disciples away and went into the mountain to pray. On the fourth night, Jesus came to the disciples by walking on the water. The disciples thought they were seeing a ghost and became afraid. And Jesus said to them, "Be not afraid, for it is I."

And Peter said to Jesus, "Lord if that's you, bid me to come to you."

And Jesus said to Peter, "Come on." And Peter stepped

out of the boat and began to walk on the water. This was impossible!

Notice that Peter was the only disciple who had enough faith to step out of that boat. He could have been hallucinating, but he had enough faith to believe that it was Jesus—until he took his eyes off Jesus and he began to sink. Be careful how you talk about Peter. I know he was lying Peter, cursing Peter, prejudiced Peter, angry Peter. But he was the only one who was willing to risk it all. Yes, he even denied the Lord. But where was he when he denied the Lord? He was right in the courtyard. He had followed Jesus to the very end, but the other disciples had gone back to their regular vocations. Their attitude was, "Let's go fishing."

What impossible situation is God challenging you to perform and to act in faith? Everything in the Bible from Genesis to Revelation has to do with faith. God says you cannot even please Him unless you come to Him in faith.

So there is an unseen world that we do not see. In Ephesians 6:12, Paul tells us there is a cosmic struggle between the force of good and evil. Satan has all of his emissaries working around the world doing his evil tasks. Hal Lindsey and Carole C. Carlson wrote a book titled *Satan Is Alive and Well on Planet Earth* (1972). The premise of their book was that Satan has been quite successful in convincing people that he does not exist. But if Satan does not exist, how do you explain evil in the world? The problem of evil has to originate from somewhere. The

. . . if Satan does not exist, how do you explain evil in the world?

Scriptures teach that men are controlled by the power of Satan.

There is a spirit at work in the world today—the spirit of Satan. He is opposed to anything that has to do with Christ. The Spirit of truth is God, and the spirit of error is the devil. The Holy Spirit's purpose is to confront the world with truth. In John 16:8, Jesus said when the Spirit comes, He will convict the world of sin, and of righteousness and of judgment. How does the Holy Spirit do this? When the church proclaims the Word of God, the Spirit of God works alongside the Word of God to bring enlightenment of sin and judgment to a lost world.

Some people seek to know the truth, and the Holy Spirit will soften their hearts to receive the truth. In Acts 16, Paul went down to the river bank where he met Lydia. As Paul began to preach, she was attentive to the Word, and God opened her heart to receive the truth.

Why does the gospel fall on deaf ears? Luke 8:5-11 says: "The seed is the Word of God, and wherever the seed is sown in the hearts of men—if they are honest—it will germinate in their hearts." Some people who go to church Sunday after Sunday hear the truth but it does not affect them. Their hearts are not receptive.

The apostle Paul, in 1 Corinthians 2:14ff, teaches about three types of men. The natural man, the spiritual man, and the carnal man. The natural man is the unsaved man who cannot receive the Spirit of God. He lives and functions by what he experiences in the natural world. He cannot comprehend the things of the Spirit because they are foolish to him. Satan has total control over his mind and he mocks God.

In 1 Corinthians 3:1, Paul teaches about the spiritual man. The spiritual man has been saved and has given his life and his will over to God. He does not live by what he sees but by what he believes. His mind has been changed. Paul says that the believer now possesses the mind of Christ.

Some believers have been converted to the faith, yet their lifestyle contradicts what they believe. 1 Corinthians 3:1-3 says that they have a carnal mind. The carnal-minded man is the man who has been saved. He has been baptized into Christ and added to the church, yet he still lives on intimate terms with the world, still thinking like the world thinks.

This is why Paul says in Romans 12:1-2: "Be not conformed to this world, but be ye transformed by the renewing of your mind." So when you come into the family of God out of a sinful life, you need to have your mind reprogrammed. Some believers are still making decisions on worldly thinking. They still think and act like the world. Eventually the carnal man will go back into the world.

Your choices may be limited, but you always have a choice.

Romans 8:5-13 says that the life the carnal man is living will eventually lead him to his death. But if his mind is controlled by the Spirit, the Spirit will lead him to life. You are the product of your choices. God made you a free moral agent. You cannot blame the results of your life on anybody else but yourself. Your choices may be limited, but you always have a choice.

The spirit of error is alive and well in the world today. It is possible for a person to be possessed by the Spirit of God and proclaim the truth. It is also possible for a person to be possessed by the spirit of the Anti-Christ and proclaim error. The believer must apply a spiritual test to what he hears. The believer must be careful to make sure that he listens to truth—and not to error.

1 Thessalonians 5:21 says: "Prove all things and hold fast to that which is good." In other words, everything you hear, see, those who you associate with, and the decisions you make must be evaluated by the Word of God. The Word of God is the only blueprint that will give you victory. The Word of God is so powerful. The Psalmist says: "Blessed is the man who walks not in the counsel of the ungodly, nor sits in the seat of the scornful, but his delight is in the law of the Lord. In His law does he meditate day and night and

he shall be like a tree planted by the rivers of waters and whatever he does he shall prosper" (Psalms 1:1-3).

Many believers are living defeated lives.

Many believers are living defeated lives. Jesus says in John 10:10: "I have come that you might have life and have it more abundantly." The question is, are you living the abundant life? In the same verse Jesus says, "the devil comes to steal, kill, and destroy." The question is, what has the devil stolen from you? Genesis 1:26 says: "God says come let us make man in our image after our likeness and let them have dominion. . . . " Man has lost his dominion. God created you to rule and reign, not be a slave.

John tells you not to believe every spirit. You have been robbed and you need to realize what the devil has taken from you, and how he has stolen it from you. He tells you not to believe every spirit. The believer should want everything that comes to him in Christ. Paul, writing to the church at Ephesus, instructs them in Ephesians 1:3 that "all spiritual blessings are in Christ." All the blessings that God has for the believer is not just spiritual.

In Matthew 6:33, Jesus further instructs you "to seek first the Kingdom of God and His righteousness and all of these things shall be added unto you." If you go back through that chapter, you will discover "things" referred to food, shelter,

The believer's future has already been prearranged by God. If you are in Christ, your ultimate destiny is determined.

clothing, money, future. The believer's future has already been prearranged by God. If you are in Christ, your ultimate destiny is determined.

It is critical that you evaluate what you hear. Test the spirit to see whether it is God. How do you do this? Acts 17:11 says: "The bereans were more noble than those in Thessalonica in that they search the Scriptures daily to see whether those things were so." So it is vitally important not only to study the Word of God to get a message to preach or teach, but study the Word of God so that you can know His will for your life.

Never compromise your spiritual devotional time with anybody. That's your time to talk to God. In 1 John 4:1ff, John gives us two groups of people. In verse 4, he says: "We are of God." In verse 5, he says: "They are of the world."

Regarding the first group, John talks about false prophets. In verse 1, he discusses the many false prophets who have gone out into the world. In verse 5, he says these false prophets are of the world, and they speak of the world, and the world hears them. Repeatedly throughout the New Testament, Jesus and the apostles warn the church concerning false prophets. Matthew 7:15 says: "Beware of false prophets who come to you in sheep clothing, but inwardly they are ravenous wolves. . . . you shall know them by their fruits."

There are people in the church who are deceptive. They are not in the church for the right reason; they are in the church to destroy it. John says: "Believe not every spirit." Notice that he connects the spirit of error with the prophets. The prophets speak what the spirit tells them to speak. The spirit here is the spirit of error, which is the spirit of the Anti-Christ who opposes Christ and His teachings.

HOW DO YOU TEST A FALSE PROPHET?

First, evaluate the content of his teaching. Check to see what he believes and teaches. Does it line up with the Word of God? In verse 3, he says: "Every spirit that does not confess that Jesus is the Christ and come in the flesh is not of God." In those days, John was dealing with the philosophy known as Gnosticism. The word "Gnosticism" comes from the Greek word "gnosis," which means "knowledge."

The Gnostics taught that all matter was evil, including humanity. And how could a righteous and holy God descend into a physical body which is evil? And so the Gnostics denied both the humanity of Christ, as well as his deity. John writes to instruct believers that what the

Gnostics were teaching was error. Today, we have people who are advocating a similar teaching.

Find out if a church or organization is a cult. You will always notice a cult by two important criteria: 1) listen to what they say about Jesus and 2) learn how they view and treat the Bible. For example, the Mormons teach that Jesus is a created being, an angel and the half-brother of Lucifer. Jehovah's Witnesses say Jesus is a created being—an angel; therefore he is less than God.

There are many other false teachings that contradict the teachings of the Word of God. So always question their teaching concerning Jesus. Second, what do they say about the Bible? Every cult will develop its own set of Scriptures to supplant the divine revelation of the Bible. The Mormons developed their own set of scriptures called *The Book of Mormon*. Jehovah's Witnesses developed their own set of scriptures called *The New World Translation* to supplant the Bible as the Word of God.

The problem with *The New World Translation* is that no reputable Hebrew or Greek scholar of biblical studies would sign his name to this version as being a reputable translation from the original text.

The New World Translation says in John 1:1: "In the beginning was the Word and the Word was with God and the Word was a god." This is in direct contradiction of what the Greek text says. The Greek text says that the Word is eternal; He was in the beginning. The text says the Word was with God showing relationship and association, and the text says the Word possesses the same divine essence and attributes that God possesses himself. The Word is *co-equal, co-eternal, and co-essence* with the Father. In John 14:1-6, Jesus says to Thomas: "When you see me you see the Father." In Hebrews 1:8, God the Father calls the Son God, thereby making the Son equal to the Father.

Many people refuse to accept the clear teaching of the Word of God. God will continue to send them truth until they are so resistant that He will not send them any more truth. In 2 Thessalonians 2:11-12, Paul says when people refuse to accept the truth, God will send them a strong delusion to make them believe a lie, when they should have believed the truth."

CHECK THEIR POPULARITY

A second way to find out if you are dealing with false prophets concerns their popularity. Do they appeal to the masses of people? Because the world recognizes their own. Because they teach what the world wants to hear. They teach themes that are soothing and pleasing to their ears. They will not teach themes that will convince and challenge people how to live. They can fill large stadiums to indoctrinate millions of people with their heretical teachings.

Prophets travel the landscape predicting and proclaiming they know the "signs of the times." They prey on the gullible, saying that certain events will transpire in their lives, and then ask them for a fee for prophesying about their lives. Many gullible believers have told me that a prophet told them something about their life. If he was not a true prophet, then how did he know certain things about me? they ask. I say, it does not take much to know something about you. It is clear in the Word of God that Satan watches and observes your behavioral patterns. He knows what your likes and dislikes are based on the choices you have made in your past.

Satan uses this information as an indicator or predictor of how you will respond and act in similar situations in the future. The Scriptures instruct that Satan has the power to influence people to think they are doing what is righteous, when, in fact, they are not (2 Corinthians 11:1-3; 2 Corinthians 12).

Satan can change himself into an angel of light. Satan has ministers who can appear as righteous ministers of the gospel when, in fact, they are not. Paul said not to be amazed that they can perform miracles. These are not authentic miracles. They are counterfeit miracles for the purpose of deception. Satan has always imitated and tried to reproduce the things of God. You should not be taken by surprise when you hear of miraculous events occurring. The only criteria you have to examine the phenomena of miracles is the Word of God.

False prophets are excellent marketers. Just look at their

attractive institutions, their cars, homes, and the clothes they wear, their private jets, and their worldwide television ministries that beam into every living room around the world. They run large publishing empires that produce their books, tapes, and CDs. To the unsuspecting believer, their doctrine must be true because they look at the success they are having by the large crowds they are drawing into their churches.

The false prophets are popular in the world and they attack the traditional church. Anybody who opposes their teaching are ridiculed as being narrow-minded, unspiritual, and heretic hunters.

COMMERCIALISM: WATCH WHAT THEY SELL YOU

False teachers know how to sell their merchandise. They exploit their followers to make material gain. But the true man of God—the people who follow Him—should be Christ-exalting, Bible-believing, and church-loving people who are not interested in material greed but interested in the Spirit of God.

In verse 6, John teaches about the second group, "We are of God." He refers to faithful preachers. How can you tell the difference between a faithful preacher and a false preacher?

A faithful preacher always agrees with the Word of God. He does not add or subtract from the Word of God because he knows there is power in the Word of God, and that he does not need to improve on what the Word of God already says. He knows clearly what Solomon says in Proverbs 30:5: "That every Word of God is pure. He is a shield to them that put their trust in Him, add thou not to His word lest he reproves thee and you will be found a liar."

Timothy knew that it was imperative for him to study the Word of God in order for him to be equipped for every good work (2 Timothy 2:15ff).

STUDY QUESTIONS

1. How does the writer describe the "unseen world"?
2. How does the author say to identify a false prophet?
3. What is the difference between the "Spirit of Truth" and the spirit of error?
4. Why does the author say it is so difficult for believers to trust God?

Chapter Two

DIVINE POWER TOWARD US

THE APOSTLE PAUL TEACHES ABOUT THE POWER THAT every believer possesses as a result of being in Christ. "That the God of our Lord Jesus Christ, the Father of glory, may give to you the spirit of wisdom and revelation in the knowledge of Him. The eyes of your understanding being enlightened; that you may know what is the hope of His calling, what are the riches of the glory of His inheritance in the saints, and what is the exceeding greatness of His power toward us who believe, according the working of His mighty power which He worked in Christ when He raised Him from the dead and seated Him at His right hand in the heavenly places" (Ephesians 1:17-20).

Paul tells the church in Ephesus of their spiritual possessions in Christ. He tells them about their adoption into the family of God, their divine election, and that God has predestined them from the foundation of the world, and how they have been sealed with the Holy Spirit of God, which is a guarantee of their inheritance and their redemption.

Paul says, "I pray that the eyes of your heart may be enlightened, illuminated. That you may know what is the hope of His calling. And what are the riches of His glory of His inheritance in the saints. And to what is the exceeding greatness of His power toward us who believe according to the working of His mighty power." What is the hope? What are the riches? And what is the exceeding greatness of His power?

As a child of God, it is important to understand the nature of hope. You live in a world that is full of despair, discouragement, and despondency. But you, as a child of God, possess the hope that Jesus will one day come and redeem you from this sinful world. You are spiritually enriched with all of God's blessings to walk in the reality of His promises.

For believers to live as God desires them to live, they need access to God's power. Verse 19 says: "The exceeding greatness of His power toward us who believe." His power can be manifested in your life. God's power was dramatically demonstrated first when He raised Jesus from the dead, which He now makes available to you. The same power that God uses to raise Jesus from the dead is the same power God has made available in your life. There are different amounts of power—but it is the same power. It would take an enormous amount of power to run an air conditioner for a large building, but you do not need the same amount of power to operate the lights in the same building. Because the power load for the paneling system could not withstand that amount of power; it would blow the system. Both systems have to use the same power source, but there are different levels of power for each system.

WHERE HAS THE POWER GONE?

The problem with the church today is it is no longer a conduit to receive God's power. She has denied the supernatural. She has denied God's power in the church. And the only way she can truly explain what is taking place in the lives of her members is the result of human reasoning. God's power can be unleashed in the church by the Holy Spirit.

The church has denied the supernatural and encounters a culture and society that emphasizes reasoning and empiricism over faith.

When I was a professor of religion, I taught a course in Catholic theology. Roman Catholicism teaches that the

The church has denied the supernatural and encounters a culture and society that emphasizes reasoning and empiricism over faith.

church has seven sacraments. The word "sacrament" means "mysterious." The sacraments are channels through which the grace of God is mediated to believers. In other words, the grace of God shows up in each of the seven sacraments, for example, the sacrament of baptism.

In the sacrament of baptism, the grace of God is expressed in the act of baptism. It is not in the water that brings about a spiritual change, but it is the grace of God that is expressed in the act of obedience. It is here that the sinner experiences God's grace. In Colossians 2:11, Paul says that "through faith, the operation of God" is at work in the act of baptism. God shows up and goes to work on the heart of the sinner—to change his old nature.

Catholicism also teaches that God shows up in the communion or the Lord's Supper. This is called "transubstantiation." When the priest blesses the bread and the wine, it no longer remains bread and wine. The bread and wine now literally become the body and blood of Jesus. In other words, Catholics believe in the supernatural and the mystery behind communion.

The problem with the contemporary church is seeing communion only as taking some crackers and grapefruit juice. No wonder people's lives have not been changed because the church has denied the reality behind the symbol. It is a mystery. That is why Paul speaks in 1 Corinthians 11:23ff concerning believers who have become weak and sick; some are asleep or have died because they did not discern the Lord's body in a worthy manner.

Martin Luther, the great leader of the Protestant Reformation in the early part of the 1500s, said when the Word of God is preached, God is heard in the proclamation of the Word. In the church's doctrinal system, we do not believe in prevenient grace. Prevenient grace is God's grace preceding any action or motion in the heart of the sinner. God's grace is effective in that it dethrones the disposition of the sinner's heart to resist His grace.

Prevenient grace is the activity of God through His word which brings enlightenment to the sinner's mind to spiritually understand God.

Prevenient grace is the activity of God through His word which brings enlightenment to the sinner's mind to spiritually understand God (1 Corinthians 2; Acts 16; John 16:8ff). In 1

Thessalonians 1:5, Paul says: "Our gospel did not come to you in word only, but in power, full assurance, and the Holy Spirit." Something happens when the Word of God is preached to bring the sinner to faith.

We have denied God's supernatural power. We have even denied the existence of a demonic world. Demonic spirits exist in the world. As the poet John Milton wrote in his famous 1667 literary piece, *Paradise Lost:* "There is a personal enemy who rules the world system. Whether you know it or not, he also influences every life to some degree. You are part of an unseen conflict in the world and within yourself. Anyone who has dominated history as he has cannot be ignored. To do will be at the peril of your very life. Millions of spirit creatures walk the earth unseen, both when we wake, and when we are asleep."

In Matthew 12:43-45, Jesus teaches about the activity of demonic spirits. First, demons can travel from place to place. They are mobile. Second, demonic spirits can live in organic creatures, animals, and humans. Third, they also can size up their victims. This spirit left the man in the text and came back and discovered that man's life had been swept cleaned. Demons can assess their victims. In the demonic realm, all demons are not the same or do not possess the same amount of power. The demon in this text decided to get seven more spirits that were worse than he was. So there is hierarchy in the demonic kingdom.

Neil Anderson, in his book titled *The Bondage Breaker*

(1990), makes a powerful statement when he says: "If you cannot explain human behavior in the categories of chemical substance abuse, prescription drugs, psychological problems, then their behavior must be attributed to demonic influence." People whom you may interact with may be under satanic power and influence. In Ephesians 2:1ff, Paul discusses this subject when he says that "there is a spirit at work in the sons of disobedience."

Hebrews 2:14 says that Jesus came to destroy Satan who had the power of death. Because Satan has been defeated and restricted does not mean that he is not at work in the world. The very problem of evil must be explained beyond simply the devious behavior of unscrupulous men.

The very problem of evil must be explained beyond simply the devious behavior of unscrupulous men.

In the Book of Job, Satan is described as walking to and fro upon the earth. God said to Satan, have you considered my servant Job? God had enough confidence in Job that he would not fail when the savage attacks of Satan would come against him. The devil will use the very person whom you are the closest to and turn your heart from God.

Job's wife said to him, "You are going through too much. You are suffering and you have prayed to God and He is silent. Why don't you just curse God and die?"

And Job responded, "You are talking like a foolish woman." This woman was frustrated because of what she saw her husband going through.

It takes divine power to tear down spiritual strongholds in your life and in the lives of others.

If you, as a believer, can realize the power that you have at your disposal, you can accomplish so much for the Lord. Many believers have spiritual strongholds in their lives they have been trying to cast down for years. They have not been successful in accomplishing this objective. It takes divine power to tear down spiritual strongholds in your life and in the lives of others.

Writing to the Corinthians (2 Corinthians 10:3-5), Paul says to the church: "For though we walk in the flesh, we do not war against the flesh. For the weapons of our warfare are not carnal but mighty in God for pulling down strongholds, casting down arguments and every high thing that exalts itself against the knowledge of God, bringing every thought into captivity to the obedience of Christ."

In Romans 1:16, Paul further teaches that the "power of God" is contained also in the gospel of Jesus Christ which is what we preach, "warning every man so that we might present every man perfect in Christ" (2 Colossians 1:28).

2 Timothy 1:7 says, "God has not given us a spirit of fear, but of power and of love and a sound mind." You, as a believer, have been endowed by the Holy Spirit to operate in the earth realm with power and authority. The question is, are you walking in your authority? God did not put you here to give you an assignment and then leave you powerless to do the job.

God did not put you here to give you an assignment and then leave you powerless to do the job.

The church has become weak and anemic to fight effectively against satanic attacks when it simply depends upon human gimmicks and intelligence. We are involved in a spiritual warfare, and we must rely upon divine power to win effectively.

Dr. David Elton Trueblood, a 20th century American theologian, in his book titled *Company of the Committed: A Manual of Action for Every Christian* (1961), once described the church as a great ship. Notice the imagery of his statement:

"The church is like a great ship upon whose deck the festivities of life of being carried on while deep below the water line a leak as been sprung and masses of water are pouring in, though the pumps are being manned night and day. While music is heard the ship is sinking hourly."

You, as a believer, must walk, act, and speak with authority.

You, as a believer, must walk, act, and speak with authority. In Matthew 28:18-20, Jesus says: "All authority in heaven and earth has been given unto me." As a believer, you operate under the authority of Christ's delegated power. You have the power of His presence; you have the power of His provision.

In Ephesians 3: 20, Paul continues to stress the power that every believer has at his disposal, "Now to Him who is able to do exceedingly abundantly above all that we ask or think, according to the power that works in us." Notice the superlatives. There is nothing in your mind that you cannot conceive that God cannot do for the believer. He works His divine power in your life.

On a piece of paper create two columns. On one side write the heading "the old man" and the other side write "the new man" to compare these two kinds of men. The old man struggles with flesh, temptations, and problems. The new man lives in God's power above his problems. The old man suffers with limited destructive efforts; he is wounded. The new man walks in a new destiny for his perfect heavenly Father. The old man deals with habitual slavery of hidden sexual sins. The new man lives like Jesus; his body is the temple of God and he tries his best to live without sin. The old man yields to sinful nature and tries to reestablish control.

The new man yields to the Holy Spirit living the abundant life in all of its fullness. The old man feels lonely, discouraged, empty, and locked into his sin. The new man experiences a loving, forgiving, and restoring relationship with Jesus. The old man is powerless to break out of demonic strongholds and bondage.

The new man breaks free of spiritual strongholds and lives in freedom and joy. The old man is spiritually impotent, immature, and unable to grow in a Christ likeness. The new man receives the indwelling of the Spirit to be empowered to live a godly life. The old man tries to develop meaningful relationships that provide stability but he can't accomplish this. The new man develops a relationship that is

The new man receives the indwelling of the Spirit to be empowered to live a godly life.

rich and stable. The old man has no support system to hold him accountable. The new man has a loving relationship that will keep him accountable to live the Christ-like life. The old man lacks vision and a life of purpose in becoming a man of God. The new man discovers God's power flowing through his mind to improve him to be more like Jesus.

The only way you can become like Jesus and overcome Satan, sin, and the flesh is to have God's divine power at work in your life. You will not have power to raise the dead, but you will have power to preach to the dead.

The believer has power to bring healing into the lives of those who need healing through the power of prayer. James 5:13ff says that the "effectual fervent prayers of the righteous accomplish much." The God of the Bible is a God of omnipotence. He is all-powerful to equip and endow you to live with power and authority to overcome everything that the enemy will bring against you.

STUDY QUESTIONS

1. Why does the author say it is vital to the believer to live by God's power?
2. What does the term "sacrament" mean?
3. What two church ordinances express the Grace of God?

4. In The *Bondage Breaker*, how does author Neil Anderson describe a person who is influenced by demonic power?
5. What is the difference between the "old man" and the "new man"?

Chapter Three

WHAT'S THAT IN YOUR HAND?

Exodus 4:1-4, 20 says: "Then Moses answered and said, 'But suppose they will not believe me or listen to my voice; suppose they say, The Lord has not appeared to you.'"

"So the Lord said to Moses, 'What is that in your hand?'"

"Moses said, 'A rod.'"

"And God said, 'Cast it on the ground.' So Moses cast it on the ground, and it became a serpent; and Moses fled from it."

"Then the Lord said to Moses, 'Reach out your hand and

take it by the tail.' (and Moses reached out his hand and caught it, and it became a rod in his hand). . . . And Moses took the rod of God in his hand."

The background of this particular passage is that God had heard the cries of His people down in Egypt. For 400 years the people of God had been under the mighty hand of Pharaoh. Now God has heard their cry and has decided the time has come to move and act. So Moses was tending his own flock and he happened to see a strange phenomenon: a bush was burning, yet the bush was not consumed.

And Moses decided to go further and to investigate this unusual phenomena. The voice of God said to Moses from the bush: "Take off your shoes, for where you stand is on holy ground." And then God said to Moses: "I have a call on your life, but not only do I have a call on your life, I have a divine assignment for your life. I want you to go down to Egypt and I want you to tell Pharaoh to let my people go."

It is interesting to note that Moses begins to make several excuses as to why he was ill-equipped and unprepared for the assignment that God had for his life. God says to Moses to quit making excuses: "I have an assignment for your life." Notice what Moses said to God: "If I go down to Egypt and the people ask me who sent me, who shall I say has sent me? I have to know who you are so I can inform Israel by what authority I come in."

Moses was no fool. Acts 7:22 says: "He was trained in all

the wisdom of the Egyptians, and he was an eloquent and educated man." Egypt was the most powerful nation on the face of the earth at that time (around the 13th century B.C.). Moses knew that Pharaoh was a powerful potentate, and Moses knew to go into the courts of Pharaoh and demand Israel be set free was absolute suicide.

Moses was asking the right questions. This was an awesome responsibility and daunting feat to lead more than 3 million people out of Egypt. Moses asked God, "You want me to lead these people? You want me to go and talk to Pharaoh?" And then Moses said to God, "First of all, who shall I say has sent me? Pharaoh and the people of Israel are going to want to know who it is who has sent me."

God said to Moses, "Tell them that I AM THAT I AM has sent you. Tell them Yahweh has sent you. Tell them El Shaddi has sent you, the almighty. Tell them that Jehovah Repphi has sent you. But when you go to them, tell them that you have the power of God behind you to do the assignment I have sent you for."

And then God said to Moses, "What is that in your hand?" Just as God had to deal with Moses, He has to deal with his people today in a similar manner. Because we constantly complain about what we do not have and what we want to have, and God tells us to use what we already have. Stop blaming other people for what you do not have. Stop blaming your social status, your environment, and your income on other factors. Stop blaming your lack of education and exposure in life as reasons for your setbacks and disappointments.

You can set the limits on your possibility and your potential. Booker T. Washington, the 19th century American Negro educator, said to the slaves when they were set free after President Lincoln's Emancipation Proclamation of January 1, 1863: "Let your buckets down where they are!" Learn to develop self-reliance and independence.

You can set the limits on your possibility and your potential.

Learn to realize that you are a child of God made in His image. You have all kinds of unique talents and possibilities. You have to pray to God and ask Him to reveal to you what your gifts and talents are. Do not try to be like someone else. You are unique and special. There is nobody else like you. God wants to do something with you because He knows you better than anybody else. How? Because He is the manufacturer.

Many people experience problems today because they have low self-esteem and inferiority complexes. God has wired you and designed you to make you unique to live out your particular potential. In the short time you are upon this planet—from the time you are born until the time you die—God expects you to use the life He has given you. Use your life to His glory and praise.

In 1 Corinthians 4:2, Paul says: "It is required of stewards that they be found faithful." Stewardship is an awesome responsibility because you do not belong to yourself—you belong to God. And God expects you to use what He has blessed you with. Discover your unique personality; discover your talents and abilities; discover your spiritual gifts which God has enabled and empowered you to use in His service for the kingdom.

When you were born, God gave you unique talents and abilities. You may not know what they are. You have to discover what they are, develop them, and deploy them in the service of God. Everybody does not have the same gifts and talents. In order for you to effectively utilize your abilities, you need to be trained, coached, developed, and to hone your gifts and talents.

In order for you to effectively utilize your abilities, you need to be trained, coached, developed, and to hone your gifts and talents.

When you were born again into the family of God by the power of the Holy Spirit, the Holy spirit not only indwells you, but He also equips and endows you with a spiritual gift to be used for the purpose of the body. So your gift will not be the same as others. Do not compare yourself to others.

Every believer has a job description given to him by the Holy Spirit. When you function according to how the Spirit has equipped you, you are going to be successful in releasing your gifts in the service of helping others and to build up the Kingdom of God.

As a believer, it is vital to your success as a Christian to understand your true purpose. When believers learn their purpose, they stay on target. So when temptations come along to derail you from your purpose, you are better prepared to deal with those distractions because you realize they do not fit into your purpose. Jesus said in John 9:4: "I must work the works of Him who sent me while it is day, for night comes when no man can work." Jesus knew that He had a divine purpose which coincided with His divine assignment. He knew he had to work within the time frame that his Father had given to him to get the job done.

As a believer, it is vital to your success as a Christian to understand your true purpose. When believers learn their purpose, they stay on target.

In the gospel of John, you will notice a recurring theme that runs throughout this gospel that is found on the lips of Jesus: "My hour has not yet come." Jesus learned to live on God's divine time table. Learn how to live on God's divine time table—no matter what people will say about you. Satan will try to get you off target. If you do not focus on Satan's plans to defeat you, his plans will come to nothing.

What's in your hand? When you discover what's in your hand, you now become accountable and responsible. You cannot blame it on anyone else if you failed to realize your purpose and the gifts God has given to you.

Understand there is a purpose for everything in God's creation. A dog functions according to its purpose. A dog does not try to act like a chicken; a cow does not try to act like bird. Their nature says what they are. You need to learn how to function according to how God has designed you. He has designed you according to your purpose.

You need to learn how to function according to how God has designed you. He has designed you according to your purpose.

You are in Christ. According to Paul in 2 Corinthians 5:17: "If any man is in Christ, he is a new creation. Old things have passed away and behold all things have become new." You now have a new purpose. You no longer are to live by the dictates of Satan and the world.

In Ephesians 2:1-4, Paul says: "You He made alive, who were dead in trespasses and sins, in which you once walked according to the course of this world, according to the prince of the power of the air, the spirit who now works in the sons of disobedience, among whom also we all once conducted ourselves in the lusts of our flesh, fulfilling the desires of the flesh and of the mind, and were by nature the children of wrath, just as the others."

In verse 5, God moves you from where you used to be to where you are now. You need to understand that your new identity is in Christ. You, as a believer, must learn not to live your life on explanations, but to live your life on the promises of God. You have to learn to walk by faith. God wants you to trust Him and to walk in His daily provision which He promised you in His word.

God expects you to build your life on His word. Jesus illustrates this point in Matthew 7:24-27 "Whoever hears these sayings of mine and does them, I will liken him into a wise man who builds his house upon a rock. The rains descends and the winds blow and beat upon your life, and it will be able to stand because it was built on a solid foundation. But whoever does not listen to these sayings of mine, I will liken him unto a foolish man who builds his house upon the sand. When the rains descend and the winds blow and beat upon his house, it will not stand because it is built on sand."

Your life can experience all that God has for you—to live in victory and power. So when the pressures of life come, you will not be defeated. The quality of your preparation determines the success of your performance. You have to train and develop your mind and spirit to think like Christ on a consistent and regular basis. You cannot wait until you are in the midst of a crisis or temptation to respond effectively.

The quality of your preparation determines the success of your performance.

You have to already have a pre-trained response to how you will respond to various situations that you may encounter. You have to decide to live your life based upon the principles of the Word of God rather than living your life based upon your passion and emotions.

STUDY QUESTIONS

1. Why does God expect believers to use what they have at their disposal?
2. How can believers take the limits of God and themselves?

3. Why is it important to have the right perspective about who you are?
4. Why is staying focused essential to believers to realize their God-given potential?

Chapter Four

YOU CAN HAVE UNSHAKEABLE FAITH

"NOW FAITH IS THE SUBSTANCE OF THINGS HOPED FOR, THE evidence of things not seen. For by it the elders obtained a good testimony. By faith we understand that the worlds were framed by the Word of God, so that the things which are seen were made of things which are visible. . . . But without faith, it is impossible to please Him, for he who comes to God must believe that He is, and that He is a rewarder of those who diligently seek Him" (Hebrews 11:1-3, 6).

Everything in the Christian religion is a matter of faith. Your faith is demonstrated by your action and by your behavior.

The writer says that without faith it is impossible to please God. Everything in the Christian religion is a matter of faith. Your faith is demonstrated by your action and by your behavior. So God requires that you operate by your faith. We live in a modern and sophisticated world where one motto seems to prevail: "I do not believe unless I see." Critics today will ridicule and criticize your faith in God. You must realize that your faith can withstand what the skeptics and the critics might say.

A critic may say, I do not live by faith. I live by what I can see. This statement is really not true. Every day many people operate their lives on the basis of what they believe. People ride in their cars, putting their complete trust in the engineers who designed these vehicles; then they drive at 75 miles per hour on the interstate. Drivers do not know whether these cars were designed according to exact specifications. Cars are subject to malfunction.

When skeptics cross a bridge, they are not sure that the civil engineers have designed that bridge according specific bridge-building codes. But they have no problem crossing a bridge that may be 40 feet above ground.

A person may need to take medication for high blood pressure or diabetes. His doctor prescribes a medication which the patient can't even read or pronounce. The pharmacist reads the unintelligible prescription and fills it for the patient who then trustingly swallows the medication according to the prescribed dosage. The patient, without even raising an eyebrow, trusts the doctor and the pharmacist. He really has faith in these two professionals. He does not have to see everything in order for him to believe that the doctor and pharmacist know what they are doing.

Everybody operates on faith so do not let any persons tell you that they do not have faith. God requires that the child of God operate on the basis of his faith.

Everybody operates on faith so do not let any persons tell you that they do not have faith. God requires that the child of God operate on the basis of his faith.

THE DEFINITION OF FAITH

Let us define the word "faith." In the New Testament, the word for "faith" is *pisitis*, which can be defined as both a verb and a noun. A verb is a state of action or being. It shows action; it has to do with believing, trusting, and reliance. Faith from the Latin word *fides* contains three elements: 1) *notitia*, which is knowledge, the actual content or information; 2) *assensus*, assent, by which the intellect acknowledges the truth of *notitia*; and 3) *fiducia*, trust, or reliance.

Faith then is the ability to trust that something exists which you do not presently see with your natural eye. It is that internal belief system planted by God in the mind of every human being which drives ordinary people to accomplish the extraordinary. Faith turns common people into uncommon achievers.

Faith turns common people into uncommon achievers.

Everybody operates on faith. Faith is your ability to trust God. Why? God will never let you down. God will work in your life. He will arrange, direct, and orchestrate your life because of your faith.

There are some key principles that will help you hold on to your faith. But remember, your faith needs to be in the right object. And the right object of your faith is in God—not in your mother, wife, husband. Your faith must be in God. In order to handle the pressures of life, you must develop your faith in God. The apostle Paul said in 2 Corinthians 5:7: "For we walk by faith and not by sight."

Remember that there are some things in life you will never understand or comprehend, but you trust that your faith will work for you.

HOW TO MAXIMIZE YOUR FAITH

Many misconceptions exist about faith. It is appropriate to examine the question about the nature faith. If you can understand what faith is, then you can learn how to maximize your faith to receive the results that God says you can have in His word.

In other words, if you can learn how to release your faith, it will transform your life. One of the greatest assets you have as a Christian is your faith because your faith is what causes God to operate supernaturally in your life.

Hebrews 11:6 says: "For it is impossible to please God, for he that cometh to God must believe that God is," that is, that He exists. "And that God is a rewarder of those that diligently seek Him."

The proof of your faith is revealed in your pursuit of the unseen.

The proof of your faith is revealed in your pursuit of the unseen. It is the inner knowing which convinces your spirit of things not seen. Faith does not depend on the aid of your five senses, and it leaves no other option which would be contrary to the Word of God.

FAITH AND THE SUPERNATURAL

Remove the supernatural from your Bible and you are left with something which has no meaning.

If you study the New Testament with an open mind, you would be compelled to acknowledge that the early Christians were permeated by the reality of the supernatural. Remove the supernatural from your Bible and you are left with something which has no meaning. When you do not see, and experience the supernatural, you have no right to speak of biblical faith.

The supernatural and the Bible are inseparably interwoven. Without the supernatural, you will have doctrine—but it will be a cold and lifeless doctrine. Doctrine must never be divorced from the supernatural. The church was born of supernatural power (Acts 2:1-47). The Christian life is a supernatural life which cannot be lived by your natural power (Galatians 2:20; 1 Corinthians 2-3; Romans 8; Galatians 5).

Prayer is supernatural communication between the believer and God for His assistance to intervene and to direct his life (James 5:13ff; Mark 11:22ff). Preaching is a supernatural event (Romans 1:16ff, 10:17; 1 Corinthians 1; 1 Thessalonians 1:5). Baptism is a supernatural event (Romans 6; Acts 2; Colossians 2:11-14). The Lord's Supper is a supernatural meal (1 Corinthians 10-11).

The indwelling presence of the Holy Spirit is a supernatural experience (Acts 2:38, 5:32; Romans 8). Spiritual warfare is a supernatural conflict (2 Corinthians 10:3; Ephesians 6:10). God's people are supernaturally protected (1 Peter 1:4; Hebrews 1:14). Unsaved people are controlled by supernatural powers—Satan and his demons (Ephesians 2:1, 6:10).

IS YOUR FAITH SUPERNATURAL?

In the 17th century, radical and revolutionary events happened that have impacted our world even to this very day. During that time a movement or spirit was born called the "Enlightenment," also called the Age of Reason.

It was a philosophical movement which stressed both reason and independence and elicited a pronounced distrust of authority. Truth was to be obtained through reason, observation, and experiment. In time, reason came to be dominated by anti-supernaturalism (such as miracles). Out of this context came biblical criticism, rejection of the idea of divine revelation, and deism (a belief that rejects the miracles of the Bible).

Its more radical forms encouraged skepticism, atheism, and agnosticism (that one cannot really know anything). The Enlightenment still lives on in secular humanism. Karl Barth, the 20th century Swiss theologian, said that the Enlightenment was "a system founded upon the omnipotence of human ability."

Many people, who believed in the Bible as the Word of God, believe that God is no longer involved with the world—or even in the world. They believe that He set the universe up like a time clock. He set the universe in motion on its own natural laws without His intervention.

Therefore the belief in the supernatural, metaphysical reality, or biblical miracles was impossible because they contradict the laws of nature or naturalism. Supernatural beings—God, angels, and demons—are outside the scope of reason and intelligence. It is impossible for the scientific mind to accept the biblical world view because it is seen simply as Hebrew folklore, myth, and legends. It is also impossible to interpret and explain natural causes (phenomenon) with spiritual explanations.

Reason is good when it comes to making natural decisions, but it emphasizes only that which can be known from the senses. This is how you know (epistemology) that reality is based on empirical data (what can be experienced tangibly). But anything beyond your senses cannot be known (metaphysical).

In the church today we have argued quite successfully through publications, lectureships, and debates about the work of the Holy Spirit. The church has downplayed, denied, or distorted the Holy Spirit's sovereign will to operate and move in the believer and in the church collectively.

The church has downplayed, denied, or distorted the Holy Spirit's sovereign will to operate and move in the believer and in the church collectively.

By not emphasizing the supernatural, everything the church does is in the realm of the natural. Our worship services have become routine, ritualistic, even with the best trained ministers who have learned the value of biblical exposition. Our churches have turned into classrooms rather than into the wonder of worship.

Look at the lives of church members and you will see no dynamic, Spirit-filled, anointed, and powerful unleashing of the Spirit. Where has the power gone? The early church experienced the anointing and empowerment of the Spirit to face a hostile, Jewish-Gentile pagan world. Would God rob us of the refreshing presence of His Spirit with power to capture the attention of the world? Without the Spirit and its power, the church has become a toothless tiger with no power to be an offense or defense. The church has no power to confront the world. It has been rendered obsolete.

How does the church explain to members—those who love the Lord and who read His word—that week after week they are fighting a loosing battle with sin? The romance of Christ is no longer attractive to them. Their lives contradict their confession.

FAITH AND YOUR MIND

Faith involves three elements of your mind. First, faith involves the intellect. It is here that you process information, and then you choose—based upon your understanding—to put your trust or confidence in the information or person.

Second, faith involves emotion. To simply process something in your mind or give intellectual assent—with no emotion or feelings to make you act—would simply be a theoretical idea of faith.

Third, faith also affects the volition that is your will. If you have faith, it will consist of all three of these elements becoming interwoven. You believe when you understand, you embrace with your heart (emotions), and you act (decide) on what you believe.

FAITH AND YOUR SENSES

Human knowledge comes from your five senses: hearing, smelling, tasting, feeling, and seeing. It is through your senses that your brain is educated about the natural world, but there are limitations to sense knowledge. You cannot know God exclusively through your senses according to Paul in Romans 1.

Your five senses are not always reliable. They can become impaired by age, stress, fear, and drugs. You cannot totally depend upon them in every situation. The natural man lives by the philosophy that "seeing is believing." He believes in the material world because he can experience it. He does not believe in God because he cannot see Him. The Word of God demands that you walk by faith; your senses demand you to walk by sight (2 Corinthians 5:7).

Since your senses have ruled you so long in your life, it is hard for them to yield their dominion to the Word of God. Walking by faith is simply walking in accordance with the Word of God. The Word of God will lead you out of the realm of your senses and into the realm of the Spirit (Romans 8:4ff).

The Word of God will lead you out of the realm of your senses and into the realm of the Spirit.

When you choose not to truly walk by faith, your mind is still receiving directions for your life from the arena of your senses. To walk by your senses *only* is to live by human reasoning and satanic counsel (1 John 2:16ff).

When you live your life through your reasoning faculties unaided by the Holy Spirit, your life will be filled by chaos and destruction because your mind is dead outside of Christ (Ephesians 2:1ff).

When you renew your mind by the Word of God, your spirit man develops and you begin to live the life God has designed for you. The natural man lives on physical food, but your spirit man (2 Corinthians 4:17) is designed to live on the Word of God. Jesus said that "man shall not live by bread alone, but by every word that proceeds out of the mouth of God" (Matthew 4:4; Deuteronomy 8:3).

God in His word reveals to your spirit man spiritual realities that you cannot see with the natural eye (Hebrews 11:1; 2 Corinthians 4:17; 2 Kings 6:14). God demands faith from you—not reason. God wants you to use your mind for His glory, but there are times when spiritual things do not make sense. For example, most religious people cannot see the importance of baptism; they do not see it as

God demands faith from you—not reason.

essential to salvation. But they miss the point when Paul says (Colossians 2:8-11) that "God operates on the heart of the believer in the act of obedience in baptism." God created you to use your mind in the natural world to accomplish your natural assignment here on earth.

FAITH AND LOGIC

Your mind functions according to logic. Logic is the systematic use of reason for inductive and deductive reasoning. Faith is total reliance on and obedience to the teachings of the Word of God. Logic will analyze and faith will act. Logic demands an explanation and faith merely needs motivation. Logic rarely produces a miracle, and faith always produces a miracle. Logic plans around what is visible, and faith plans on what is invisible.

WHY HAVE FAITH?

First, it is impossible for you to please God. God wants you to trust Him and rely upon Him even though you cannot see Him (2 Corinthians 4:17). In Romans 4:17, when God called Abraham and told him to offer up his only begotten son, Isaac, Abraham so trusted God that he was willing to obey what God had said. To approach God, you must have faith.

Second, it is impossible for you to win this spiritual conflict. You need faith. Paul said in Ephesians 6:10 to take on the shield of faith and to fight the good fight of faith.

THE BENEFITS OF YOUR FAITH

First, according to Romans 5:2, faith produces hope. If you do not have faith, you cannot have hope. When problems arise in your life, you need to have hope, and hope is based upon faith in God. It is based upon faith in His word. It is based on faith in His promises.

Second, faith produces joy. Do you want joy in your life? In the midst of every circumstance and every problem you face, you need to have faith. You don't trust your circumstances, and you don't trust in human beings or your financial situation, but you believe God because God is the one who produces joy in your heart.

Third, Romans 15:13 talks about how faith produces peace in your life. You can trust God when it seems as if everything is going wrong. You know He produces hope, joy, and peace and that you may abound in the power of the Holy Spirit.

Fourth, your faith will produce confidence. 1 Peter 2:6 says that you can have confidence. You can know that God is with you to work everything out according to His divine will.

Fifth, faith can produce boldness (2 Corinthians 4:13). Some people may think that you are arrogant. Some people may think that you are full of pride. But when you have faith, you do not allow your problems to overwhelm you. No one can take away your peace, your joy, your hope, your boldness because they came from God. These positive benefits come as a result of your faith in Him.

FAITH IS A CHANNEL

Faith is also the channel that makes God's possibilities available to you. Jesus says in Mark 10:27: "Some things are impossible with men, but with God, all things are possible." If you want the provisions of God available in your life, they must come through the channel of faith.

Faith is also the channel that makes God's possibilities available to you.

VISIBLE TO THE INVISIBLE

Your faith allows you to see beyond the visible to the invisible. You cannot see spiritual realities with your natural eye, but this does not mean the spiritual world does not exist. You have to believe and confess what God has said in His word, and it will manifest itself in your life. That's why Jesus said in Mark 11:22ff "that whatever you say, believe you shall receive them."

Faith precedes physical sight. If you have to see something in order to believe it exists, then you really do not have faith. You believe in many things, but you cannot see them. You believe in electricity, but you cannot see it. You believe in the wind, but you cannot see it. You see only its manifestation. Paul says in 2 Corinthians 5:7: "We walk by faith and not sight." The Christian acts on the Word of God.

FAITH AND BEHAVIOR

Faith links your behavior directly to God, and it affects every area of your life, such as your finances, marriage, career. It affects every aspect of your life.

ORIGIN OF FAITH

Remember your faith does not originate with you but with God. It is God who produces faith (Romans 10:17; 12:3).

THE RIGHT KIND OF FAITH IS THE RIGHT AMOUNT OF FAITH

If you, as a believer, can have the right kind of faith the size of a mustard seed, it will be sufficient to make mountains move in your life. What mountains do you have in your life that you need to move? As a Christian, according to Galatians 2:20, "You live by faith." Romans 16:20 says: "You stand by faith." Do not let loose your faith! Stand by faith!

Did you know, according to Ephesians 6:16 and 1 Peter 5:9, you defeat the devil by your faith? Did you know, according to 1 Peter 1:9, you must develop your faith? Peter said add virtue to your faith. That's the key. You must develop your faith.

THE OBJECT OF YOUR FAITH

Your faith should not be in men but in Christ (Acts 20:21). Your faith should be in God (Hebrews 11:6; John 14:1). When Jesus departed to go back to heaven, He said to his disciples: "Let not your heart be troubled. You believe in God, believe in me also. In my Father's house are many mansions. If it were not so, I would not have told you. I'm going to prepare a place for you" (John 14:1-6)

You must believe in God. You must believe in the Holy Spirit. He is your comforter He dwells in you, He guides you, and He teaches you according to the Word of God. You must develop your faith in the promises of God. Do not let anybody tell you that His word is insufficient for "all Scripture is given by the inspiration of God."

The Bible is the mind of God. His word can be trusted. Proverbs 30:5 says: "Every Word of God is pure and He is a shield to them that put their trust in Him add not to His word lest He reprove you and you be found a liar."

Trust in Christ, in God, in the Spirit, and in the Word of God, which is the will of God for your life. When you do this, you are relying upon the promises of God. Peter said in 2 Peter 1:3-4 that God's promises are great. When you trust in your own power rather than God, you are setting yourself up for failure.

WALKING BY FAITH

In 2 Corinthians 5:7, the apostle Paul says: "We walk by faith and not by sight." Faith means to have confidence and trust in God. Whatever it may be that God wants you to do, He wants you to operate in faith on His word. Thus, faith is necessary because faith challenges you to believe that God will reward you. Hebrews 11:6 says that faith pleases God. If you are going to be victorious in spiritual warfare, you must have the shield of faith to deflect the arrows of the evil one (Ephesians 6:13-16).

PRAYER AND FAITH

The Bible consistently emphasizes the unique and supreme importance of faith. Faith is exclusively related to two realties you cannot see with your natural eye: God and His spiritual provisions that are revealed in the Word of God.

Prayer is an exercise of your faith. Without faith, there is no assurance of future blessings. Your victory as a believer in life does not depend upon fate; it depends on your faith.

Prayer is an exercise of your faith. Without faith, there is no assurance of future blessings.

James says in James 1:5: "If any man lacks wisdom, let him ask God who gives to all generously and without reproach, and it will be given to him. But he must ask in faith without doubting, for the one who doubts is like the waves of the sea, driven and tossed by the wind. For that man ought not to expect that he will receive anything from the Lord."

For your prayers to be effective and to bring results you must remember the following principles:

First, remember that God moves and operates on faith. Hebrews 11:6 says: "For he that cometh to God must believe that God exists, and that God is the rewarder of those who diligently seek him."

Second, James 5:17-18 says that prayer in faith has the power to move God to act on your behalf. Prayer is a petition to God, for Him to show up in your life, to change, arrange, control, direct, and orchestrate situations in your life.

The power of faith in prayer is the confidence of the intervention of the supernatural favor of God in your life. He will give you power to do tasks that you cannot accomplish on your own. You need God's help.

Third, the prayer of faith is the power to believe that you have received what you have asked for. The believer knows that what he has received by faith will in due season be manifested in his life. It's the prayer of faith that sees the fulfillment before it happens.

You can receive by faith when you pray, but the granting of your desires still remains in the future.

You can receive by faith when you pray, but the granting of your desires still remains in the future.

You know by faith—that you have received now in the Spirit—what God has granted to you. You know that God has His own appointed time for things you have received at the moment of praying when He will actually grant those things to you in the natural or physical realm.

Fourth, prayer demonstrates that God is faithful to His children, and that He will respond to their needs. Psalms 34:8 says: "O taste and see that the Lord is good; how blessed is the man who takes refuge in Him, O fear the Lord, you His saints, for to those who fear Him there is no want. . . . But they who seek the Lord shall not be in want of any good thing." Psalms 84:1 says: "No good thing does He (God) withhold from those who walk uprightly."

THE EFFECTS OF THE PRAYER OF FAITH

1. The key to obtaining what you ask from God is to receive it by faith at the very moment you petition him.
2. When you pray, it sets you free from continual struggle and anxiety, and praying brings you an inner peace that something will be done.
3. The receiving of your request is your part of the transaction, but the manifestation is God's part.
4. The results of your prayer are guaranteed when they are in line with the Word of God—His will (1 John 5:14; 2 Corinthians 1:20).

THE PROBLEM OF UNBELIEF

1. **You make God a liar.** You do not believe that God will do what He says He will do. (Numbers 23:19; Isaiah 55; Jeremiah 1:12).

2. **You question the dependability and the integrity of the Word of God.** The believer walks in the assurance that the Word of God is true (Hebrews 4:12; Romans 1:16; Proverbs 30:5).
3. **Unbelief wastes time.** Because you do not trust and walk in the assurance of who God is, you will never accomplish God-given dreams that He has assigned for you.
4. **It robs you of God's blessings.** When you should be walking in the favor of God, you are walking in defeat, depression, and anxiety.
5. **God is limited by what He can do for you because of your unbelief.** God will not act or bring results in your life if you do not open up the possibility for His grace to work in your life.

FAITH AND THE WORD OF GOD

In Romans 10:17, Paul says that faith is produced by the Word of God, which means that every believer needs to take the time to really appreciate, study, and analyze what the Word of God says.

It is absolutely paramount that believers need the Bible for their spiritual development and spiritual growth. Paul, in 2 Timothy 3:16, says that "all Scripture is given by the inspiration of God, and it is profitable for doctrine, profitable for reproof, and correction, and training in righteousness, that the man of God may be thoroughly equipped unto every good work."

The believer's previous experiences with God will validate tomorrow's expectations. In other words, if you have walked with God and you have seen Him at work in your life, you know that there were doors opened that could not have been opened except by the grace and mercy of God.

Your experiences every day ought to draw you closer to God. Paul says in Romans 11:20 that you should stand on your faith. The devil will come and he will do his very best to move you away from the very promises of God.

There are times in your life when you may not understand what God is doing. For everything God has in store for you, we have to walk in faith, trusting that God is in control. God knows what He is doing in your life. You cannot defeat the devil unless you defeat him by your faith.

You cannot defeat the devil unless you defeat him by your faith.

You have to learn to hold on to God. Times may be difficult. You may have pain and sorrow in your life. But the believer does not worry about the circumstance of life he may encounter. He asks God to give him the grace not to necessarily change the circumstances, but to give him the grace to work through every circumstance in his life.

THE MEASURE OF FAITH

Jesus talked about the measure of your faith. In Matthew 8:26, He spoke about having faith the size of a mustard seed to move mountains in your life.

In Romans 14, believers have been instructed to bear the infirmities of the weaker brother because the weaker brother is weak in faith. Every believer is not on the same level. The way you grow and develop your faith is to take the Scriptures and digest them, study them, and meditate upon biblical truths for your enrichment and edification.

In 1 Corinthians 15:7, Paul says that he declared to the Corinthians the gospel by which they were saved if they would keep in memory what he had preached unto them, lest they had believed in vain. Your faith can become worthless because you have rejected the object of your faith, who is God.

The facts of the gospel are so powerful that they can radically change your life if you surrender in faith to God. Are you standing on your faith to believe?

WHERE WILL YOUR FAITH LEAD?

A life of faith is a life of trust. Trusting in what? Trusting that God works in every circumstance. In John 5:4, the apostle John says the life that you live as a believer is a life of victory! You are more than a conqueror through Jesus

Christ. Why are you not living your life on the basis of your faith? Your faith should be the compelling force in your life. If you lose your faith, you are defeated.

Faith is absolutely essential for you to live as a believer. Remember that as a believer, your action and behavior is based on the Word of God when there is no physical evidence in sight that your behavior is correct.

FAITH AND YOUR CONFESSION

Every believer should possess a powerful, positive, and dynamic confession. The word "confession" comes from the Greek word "homo-lego," meaning to speak the same or to agree. Hebrews 3:1ff says Jesus is the High Priest of our confession (profession).

Jesus went to Calvary to die for you that you might be justified in the eyes of God. He went to Calvary to claim divine privileges that God now makes available to you.

Jesus went to Calvary . . . to claim divine privileges that God now makes available to you.

Many believers do not live the life Christ died to give them. In John 10:10, Jesus says, "I have come that you might have life, and have it more abundantly." The abundant life is the life that

Christ makes available to you if you come to Him in faith and surrender to His will.

In 2 Corinthians 5:14, Paul says: "For the love of Christ controls us, having concluded this that one died for all, therefore all died; and He died for all, so that they who live might no longer live for themselves, but for Him who died and rose again on their behalf."

Jesus became poor that you might become rich. As a believer, you can live a dynamic life by the power of the indwelling presence of the Holy Spirit, to walk in divine victory. When Jesus died, He instituted the New Testament (Covenant,). The Hebrew writers say that Christ is the guarantee of a better covenant. Jesus guaranteed every promise in the New Covenant. You must begin to walk in the reality of those promises.

The final authority in your life over every situation you may encounter is the Word of God.

The final authority in your life over every situation you may encounter is the Word of God. You need to constantly fill your mind with the Word of God.

HINDRANCES TO YOUR FAITH

First, fear intimidates and robs you of your blessings. In John 10:10, Jesus says that the devil comes to steal, kill, and destroy. In John 8:44-45, Jesus again warns us that "the devil is a murderer, a liar, and the father of lies." Satan is not omnipotent and all-powerful. He is not "omnipresent." He cannot be everywhere at one time. Satan is not "omniscience." He does not know everything. He is limited and powerless because Jesus defeated him at the cross.

You can begin to walk in the reality that Satan is a defeated foe. He will go around seeking those whom he may devour (1 Peter 5:8). He will try to scare you, lie to you, out-scheme you, and tempt you. But the Bible says you can resist him and give him no place of opportunity. Beware of his devices. He is successful because he blinds the minds of unbelievers to keep them from seeing the truth. In 2 Timothy 1:7, Paul says: "God has not given you a spirit of fear, but of power and a sound mind."

Second, what others say about you. Do not let others define who you are. You are a child of God, a joint-heir, and you are a conqueror in Christ. Let others talk about you, but keep on speaking the Word of God over them.

Third, fact knowledge versus faith knowledge. Fact knowledge says your circumstances dictate how you will speak and behave.

As a believer, you have been born again by the power of the Holy Spirit. You no longer operate on the basis of what you see, but operate on the basis of your faith. You live by faith—not by your sight (2 Corinthians 5:7). The natural man looks at his circumstances and he allows them to control him. This is fact knowledge.

Faith knowledge is produced on the basis of the Word of God. In Romans 10:17, Paul says that "faith comes by hearing, and hearing by the Word of God." When faith is produced by the Word of God, then you walk by the Word of God because it empowers you to be victorious. When you have learned to trust God, and not your circumstances, your faith in God, will move mountains out of your path. Learn to confess and agree with what God says about your life in His word.

There are no circumstances or situations that God will not give you power to overcome. He will give you every resource you need. But you have to activate and maximize your faith. He will give you peace (Philippians 4:7). He will give you power (Philippians 4:13). He will give you provisions to meet all of your needs (Philippians 4:19).

There are no circumstances or situations that God will not give you power to overcome.

You will either believe the Word of God to produce faith or you will never live in the provisions of blessings God has for you.

Jesus says in Matthew 10:32: "Whoever is afraid to confess me before men, I will be ashamed to confess you before my Father." Confess Jesus as Lord, that He is your High Priest. Confess that He has the power to meet your every need when you maximize your faith!

When you speak the Word of God, your confession will reveal your faith, conviction, and hope. Negative and faithless talk will destroy your faith. Faithless talk always produces a faithless walk.

You will either believe the Word of God to produce faith or you will never live in the provisions of blessings God has for you.

FAITH PRINCIPLES TO KEEP IN FOCUS

1. You must know what you want before your faith can target it.
2. God promotes and rewards you according to your progressive acts of obedience.
3. God cannot commit himself to the success of a rebel.
4. You will inevitably experience what you consistently expect.

STUDY QUESTIONS

1. Why is faith so important in the life of every believer?
2. How does the writer define the word "faith"?
3. Why is faith and the supernatural so important?
4. What is the "Enlightenment?"
5. What is "epistemology"?
6. What is "metaphysical"?
7. What is "sensory mechanism"?
8. What are the five benefits of having faith?
9. Why does the author say that faith is channeled?
10. Why is it important that your conversation should reveal your faith walk?

Chapter Five

THE BATTLE FOR THE MIND

In Romans 7:14-21, the apostle Paul deals with four laws, as they relate in winning the battle for the mind. The first law is the law of God. God revealed His law to the children of Israel in Exodus 20 after He brought them out of Egypt to the base of Mount Sinai, where He gave them the Ten Commandments. The Ten Commandments revealed God's holiness.

The second law is the law of your members. Your body is controlled by law. The third law is the law of the mind. The law of the mind directs the law of your members to fulfill the desires of the mind. The fourth law is the law of sin and death which is the carnal nature of man, which is contrary to the will of God. The carnal nature is to live independently of God's expectation. So, the dilemma Paul finds himself in, on the one hand, is to serve the law of God with his mind, and on the other hand, to fulfill his carnal desire by following the law of sin and death. He finds himself pulled in either direction. If the law of the mind is influenced either by the law of God or the law of sin, the body will manifest the desire of either one.

If the law of the mind is influenced either by the law of God or the law of sin, the body will manifest the desire of either one.

Paul said, he was in a terrible situation. "O wretched man that I am, who will deliver me from this body of death?" Every human being is involved in this spiritual warfare. It is different from any other war that that has been fought on the battlefields of the world. It is a spiritual, cosmic warfare between God and Satan.

The war has already been won by Jesus Christ on the cross. The church has been given the assignment to enforce the victory which has been won. This warfare takes place in the minds of men who are blinded to the truth of God's word. Every person possesses a belief system. A belief system is a cognitive map of how we understand the world around us. It is how we make decisions; it determines our value system.

Your belief system determines your behavior. If you can change your beliefs, you can change your behavior. Your walk as a Christian is directly related to what you believe about God. The longer you hold on to an unbiblical belief system, the success of your daily walk of faith will be dismal at best. Your belief system determines our behavior.

Your belief system determines your behavior. If you can change your beliefs, you can change your behavior.

Satan's desire is to influence you to develop a belief system which will produce ungodly behavior. In 2 Corinthians 4:1ff, Paul said that Satan blinds the minds of men to keep them from obeying the truth. The battle for the mind is a conflict between God's way of living or Satan's way of living, which is to live by the desires of the world and of the flesh. We are the only ones who will determine the winner in this battle.

The battle for the mind is clearly seen in Romans 7:14-25: the first thing to know is that this battle is not fought on the level of human ability. The believer must realize that he cannot out-think or out-muscle the devil by his own power. The believer's weapons must be divine in order to win this spiritual conflict.

STRONGHOLDS

In 2 Corinthians 10:3-5, Paul said, "For the weapons of our warfare are not flesh but of divine power to destroy strongholds, taking every thought captive to the obedience of Christ." What is a stronghold? A stronghold is a belief system which has developed in your mind through repetition over a period of time. How are strongholds established in the mind? God has designed you to live in fellowship with Him to fulfill His purposes for your life, but when you were born, we were born physically alive and spiritually dead in a world that is opposed to God's value system.

A stronghold is a belief system which has developed in your mind through repetition over a period of time.

In Ephesians 2: 1-2, Paul said that "we were dead in our sins and in our trespasses, but God made us alive. Before God saved you, you lived according to the course of this world and the philosophy and ideas of this world. You lived according to the prince of the power of the air. There was a spirit that influenced and controlled us as the child of disobedience. You wonder why some people do what they do. It is because they have a "spirit of disobedience." Before you came to Jesus Christ, all your experiences came from your sinful environment.

You were influenced and shaped by the world systems which influenced your parents, teachers, friends, and spouses. The world system has influenced and impacted your thinking by the places you lived, the schools you attended, and the books, magazines, and newspapers you read.

In addition, media outlets, such as television and movies, have also influenced your thinking. The music you listen to has influenced you. The world has its own culture and language. That is why the apostle Paul said in Romans 12:1-2, "I beseech you therefore, brethren, by the mercies of God, that you present your bodies a living sacrifice, holy, acceptable unto God, which is your reasonable service. And be not conformed to this world: but be transformed by the renewing of your mind, that you may prove what is the good, and acceptable, and perfect will of God."

Whenever you feel attracted to leave God's purpose and plan for your life, you are experiencing a temptation.

The world wants to mold you into its belief system. The world wants you to adopt its philosophy and its value system. When you became a Christian, your old ways of thinking and behaving should have changed when you were taught the gospel and submitted your life to Christ. Your belief system is not to be conformed to this world but to be transformed by the renewing of your mind. Whenever you feel attracted to leave God's purpose and plan for your life, you are experiencing a temptation.

TEMPTATION

The purpose of a temptation is to get you to fulfill genuine, authentic needs through the world system which controls you rather than through Christ (1 John 2:15ff). That is where the real battle is. In James 1:13, James said, "Let no man say when he is tempted, I am tempted by God. God cannot be tempted with evil, neither tempts he any man: but every man is tempted, when he is drawn away of his own lust, and enticed. Then when lust hath conceived, it brings forth sin: and sin, when it is finished, brings forth death."

So, you are drawn by your own temptations to leave the will of God. Paul said in 1 Corinthians 10:13, "There hath no temptation taken you but such as is common to man; but God is faithful, who will not suffer you to be tempted above that which you are able; but will with the temptation also make a way to escape, that you may be able to bear it." All you have to do is be led by the Spirit through His word to look for the exit signs to get out of the temptation.

John said in 1 John 2:15ff, "Love not the world, neither the things of the world for they are the lust of the flesh and the lust of the eyes and the pride of life." These are the three avenues in which Satan baits you to leave the will of God. The devil has watched your behavior over the years and he knows where you are weak and that is where he attacks you.

That is why you have to stay firm in the Word of God. The moment you are tempted, you are on the threshold of a decision. If you do not choose to take captive your thoughts and make them obedient to Christ, we will consider the temptation as an option, and our emotions will be affected in the likelihood of yielding to that temptation. You can take control over your minds by having your minds renewed in the image of Christ.

The moment you are tempted, you are on the threshold of a decision.

The Bible teaches that God has provided a way of escape from every temptation. If you do not control your thoughts, you will run the risk of allowing the temptations to control you. Any wrong thinking you cannot control will produce a stronghold in your life. Somewhere in your past, you have formed a habit or a pattern of thinking that now controls you. In order to win the battle for your mind, you need divine empowerment. If your mind has been programmed incorrectly, it can be reprogrammed by listening and studying the Word of God.

Psalms 1:1-3 says: "Blessed is the man who does not walk in the counsel of the ungodly, nor stands in the way of the sinners, nor sits in the seat of the scornful. But his delight is in the law of the Lord; and in his law doth he mediate day and night. And he shall be like a tree planted by the rivers of water that bring forth his fruit in his season; his leaf also shall not wither; and whatsoever he doeth shall prosper." God told Joshua, "If you want to be successful in taking the land of Canaan, I want you to meditate on the Word of God day and night, and do not depart to the right or to the left" What you think about controls your speech and controls your behavior.

You are also up against the devil who is scheming to fill your mind with thoughts which are opposed to God's will for your life. Satan will put his thoughts and ideas into your mind to deceive you into believing that they are yours. Remember the incident recorded in Acts 5: 1-13 about how Ananias lied to Peter concerning the land which they had sold for a certain amount of money. Peter said, "Why have you lied to the Holy Spirit?"

John 13:27 says that when Judas was to betray the Lord,

Satan had already entered into his heart. Satan will get into your heart and make you think that what you are doing is what you really want to do. He will make you think that it is your thoughts. How does he do this? If Satan can get you to believe a lie, he can control your life. That is how he deceived our parents, Adam and Eve. Satan has no power over you except what you give to him. You can resist the devil and he will flee from you. Paul warns that you should not be ignorant of Satan's devices, but you should put on the armor of God so that you may be able to stand against Satan.

Satan's primary weapon against you is a lie, and your defense against him is the truth. Jesus said in John 8:31-32, "If you continue in my word, then truly you are my disciples, you shall know the truth and the truth shall set you free." When Satan comes at you with a lie, you need to be able to take the sword of the Spirit—the Word of God—to defeat him. In Deuteronomy 8:12, God says that "man shall not live by bread alone but by every word that proceeds out of the mouth of God." You have authority as a believer to have dominion in every area of your life.

Satan's primary weapon against you is a lie, and your defense against him is the truth.

When you expose Satan's lies with God's truth, his power is broken.

When you expose Satan's lies with God's truth, his power is broken. In John 17:17, Jesus said, "Sanctify them in thy truth, thou word is truth." According to Colossians 1:13, "We have been translated out of the kingdom of darkness into the Kingdom of God's dear Son." No longer are you under Satan's control and directives for your life. Now, you are living by the power of Christ.

WHAT IS OUR PART IN THIS BATTLE?

First, you are going to have to learn how to transform your thinking. You have to reprogram your mind. Many believers in the church are still making decisions based on their old way of thinking rather than having the mind of Christ. If you are going to be like Christ, you have to think like Christ.

Second, you must renew your mind every day by filling it with the Word of God. In Philippians 4:8, Paul said to think on these matters. "Whatever is good and noble, praiseworthy and honest of good report, think on these things."

Third, you must let Christ rule your heart. Colossians 3:15-16 says, "Let the Word of Christ dwell in you richly in all wisdom; teaching and admonishing one another in psalms and hymns and spiritual songs, singing with grace in your hearts to the Lord. And whatever you do in word or deed, do all in the name of the Lord Jesus, giving thanks to God and the Father by Him." Not only must your mind be changed and filled with the Word of God, but Christ must rule in your hearts.

Fourth, you must let the Word of Christ fill your mind with God's truth so you will equip yourself to recognize Satan's lies and take those thoughts captive to the obedience of Christ. Peter said in I Peter 1:13, "You must prepare your mind for action." When a thought does not agree with the Word of God, you have to resist it right away and choose to believe and act on the truth.

When a thought does not agree with the Word of God, you have to resist it right away and choose to believe and act on the truth.

Fifth, you have to turn to God in prayer. Philippians 4:6 says "His peace will guard our hearts," and when you need strength to make it. Philippians 4:13 says that "you can do all things through Christ who strengthens you."

Sixth, you must assume absolute total responsibility for your thoughts. Philippians 4:8-9 says what you think about the most is what controls you. You must assume responsibility for your thoughts. Victory in the battle for your mind is an inheritance you have in Jesus Christ. You have victory—the battle has been won.

THE POWER OF CHOICE

Choices you make will result in consequences that you will reap.

If you are going to be victorious, you have to know how to make good decisions. God created you as a free moral agent, a free moral agent with the capacity to make choices. Choices you make will result in consequences that you will reap. "For whatever a man sows, that shall he also reap." If you plant seeds of destruction, you will reap a harvest of destruction. You have to ask God to give you wisdom to make good decisions because godly decision-making is based on how you have been trained to think. There is a link between what you think and the decisions you make. When you make natural decisions based on the flesh, rather than for God, you will experience pain. But when you make godly decisions, you experience God's blessings in your life.

When you make godly decisions based on God's word, you trigger the supernatural power of God to bring it to pass. What stands between you and your victory as a believer is your ability to make good decisions. To improve the quality of your decision, you must change the way you think.

RENEWING THE MIND

This is done when you renew your mind. Your mind is composed of a conscious and a subconscious mind. The conscious mind processes information. If the conscious mind accepts this information as true, it is stored in your filing system which is your subconscious mind.

The way your mind becomes renewed is by changing the old information which is stored in your subconscious mind with the Word of God.

Decisions are evaluated by your subconscious mind where previous information you have accepted to be true is stored. You automatically make your decisions based on your subconscious mind. The way your mind becomes renewed is by changing the old information which is stored in your subconscious mind with the Word of God.

You can change your thinking because God has given you the power to do so. Satan has no advantage over you.

You must learn how to reprogram your thinking. You cannot be controlled by your senses—what you see, taste, touch, and smell. You have to operate your life based on what is God's will for your life. Because your mind has been programmed with a host of unscriptural ideas, it is not enough to put new information into your mind. You must also release the old unscriptural information by feeding your mind on the Word of God. You will develop a new belief system which will result in a new behavior—and a new person.

Fulfilling God's plan for your life requires the ultimate transformation from the world's way of thinking to God's way of thinking. It takes the renewing of your mind. Will your mind be controlled by the law of God or by the law of sin and death? That is the question that must be answered.

STUDY QUESTIONS

1. What are the four spiritual laws the author mentions?
2. What is a belief system?
3. What is a stronghold?
4. What is the world system?
5. What are three specific ways the world's system influences us?
6. What is the author's definition of temptation?

7. What is Satan's weapon against believers and non-believers?
8. Why is making good decisions so important to changing behavior?
9. What is the difference between the conscience and subconscious mind?

Chapter Six

SEATED IN AUTHORITY

JESUS HAS WON VICTORY FOR YOU AND LED SATAN AND his demonic cohorts into captivity. Satan is a defeated foe. As a believer, you must realize that you have the power and the victory in Jesus Christ. "Even when we were dead in our sins, hath quickened you together with Christ, (by grace ye are saved); And hath raised us up together, and made us sit together in heavenly places in Christ Jesus: That in the ages to come he might show the exceeding riches of his grace in his kindness toward us through Christ Jesus" (Ephesians 2:5-8).

In the first chapter of the Book of Ephesians, Verses 20-23, Paul said that God "worked in Christ when He raised him from the dead and sat Him at His own right hand in the heavenly places for above all principalities and powers and mighty dominion in every name that is named not only in this world, but also in the world to come. He had put all things under His feet and gave Him to be head over all things to the church which is His body of the fullness of Him that filleth all in all."

Jesus is now sitting at the right hand of the Father and has been given all authority in His hand (Matthew 28:19-20).

SEATING ARRANGEMENTS

Seating arrangements in the ancient world have always been significant and political. Seating positions have always been noted as a degree of honor or lack thereof. Having completed His work of redemption on the cross, Jesus is now seated at the right hand of God.

Having completed His work of redemption on the cross, Jesus is now seated at the right hand of God.

Hebrews 1:1-4 says: "God, who at sundry times and in diverse manners spoke in time past unto the fathers by the prophets, Hath in these last days spoken unto us by His Son, whom He hath appointed heir of all things, by whom also He made the worlds; Who being the brightness of His glory, and the express image of His person, and upholding all things by the word of His power, when He had by himself purged our sins, sat down on the right hand of the Majesty on high."

When Jesus accomplished the work that God had sent Him to accomplish, He is now sitting at the right hand of the Father. The right hand symbolizes the place given to the most favored guest, signifying a place of honor, dignity, and power. Thus the right hand was a mark of the highest honor of exhortation and authority. Christ—by virtue of His person—is God manifested in the flesh. He co-existed, co-equaled, and was co-eternal with the Father. He went down into the earth-realm and took on human nature (John 1:14). And now He is restored to his place of sovereignty (1 Corinthians 15:24-28; John 17:2-5).

The believer shares in His resurrection. Romans 6:1-4 says: "What shall we then say? Shall we continue in sin, that grace may abound? God forbid. How shall we, that are dead to sin, live any longer therein? Know ye not, that so many of us as were baptized into Jesus Christ were baptized into His death? Therefore we are buried with Him by baptism into death: that like as Christ was raised up from the dead by the glory of the Father, even so we also should walk in the newness of life."

When you were raised with Jesus in the ceremonial waters of baptism, you ascended with Christ into heaven.

As a believer, you have become a new person. Old things are passed away and behold all things have become new. Paul said that you died when you were crucified with Christ. No longer do you live, but it is Christ who lives in you. The life that you now live, you live by the faith of the Son of God who loves you and gave himself for you (Galatians 2:70). When you were raised with Jesus in the ceremonial waters of baptism, you ascended with Christ into heaven.

You are sitting in honor with Christ in the heavenly realm. This elevation of the believer is now seated in authority with Him. You were made to sit with Him as heirs and joint-heirs with Christ.

You are sitting with Christ in heaven, and all things are subject unto you. That means that Satan has been defeated. Hebrews 2:14: "Forasmuch then as the children are partakers of flesh and blood, He also himself likewise took part of the same; that through death He might destroy him that had the power of death, that is the devil; and deliver them who through fear of death were all their lifetime subject to bondage." You have a High Priest who is made like you who can come to you in your very time of need.

John said in 1 John 3:9-10: "Whosoever is born of God doth not commit sin; for his seed remains in him: and he cannot sin, because he is born of God." Verse 8: "He that commits sin is of the devil: for the devil sin from the beginning. For this purpose the Son of God was manifested, that he might destroy the works of the devil."

You have authority over the kingdom of darkness. Colossians 1:13: "Who hath delivered us from the power of darkness, and hath translated us into the kingdom of His dear Son." This means that Satan no longer has power over your life. Satan no longer controls the strings in your life.

You have authority over the kingdom of darkness.

According to Paul in Ephesians 1:19, "The eyes of your understanding being enlightened; that ye may know what is the hope of His calling, and what the riches of the glory of his inheritance in the saints. And what is the exceeding greatness of His power to us who believe, according to the working of His mighty power, which He wrought in Christ, when He raised Him from the dead, and set Him at His own right hand in the heavenly places."

The same power that God used when He raised Jesus from the dead is the same power we have available to you. All you have to do is walk in divine power. Why? Because you have divine victory. 2 Peter 1:3: "According to His divine power, He has given unto us all things that pertain to life and godliness." You have the same power. Do you have the same amount of power? No! But you have the same power. Your identity as a child of God and your authority is something you possess now.

Satan's defeat is not pending and it is not something in the future. It has already happened. It is not your responsibility to defeat him. Jesus has already done that. You are qualified to have authority.

QUALIFIED FOR AUTHORITY

As a believer, you are qualified to have authority and to sit on the right hand of God for five reasons. First, John 1:12: "Jesus came unto His own and His own received Him not, but as many as received Him, He gave them the authority to become the sons of God or the children of God. "Those who believe in His name have authority because they are the children of God."

Second, according to Ephesians 1:19, you have been qualified for authority because of your faith. When you have enough faith to believe that Jesus is the Son of God, and to surrender your life to Christ. God empowered you as His child.

Third, you have been qualified for authority because of your humility. Humility is confidence properly placed. It is not because of anything that you have done. It is because of what Jesus has done.

Ephesians 1:3 says: "All spiritual blessings are in Christ Jesus." As long as you are in Christ, you are more than a conqueror. Nothing can separate you from the love of Christ. Neither tribulation, persecution, famine, death, nor peril should separate you from Christ.

Fourth, you are qualified for authority because you have boldness. In Joshua 1: 6-8, God tells Joshua to have boldness and courage, because if you are going to be victorious in this spiritual warfare, you have to be bold. God cannot use cowards. God needs believers who are risk-takers, believers who are willing to venture out in faith because they are sure of the outcome. They trust God for the outcome.

God needs believers who are risk-takers, believers who are willing to venture out in faith because they are sure of the outcome.

In Acts 4:31, when Peter and John stood before the Sanhedrin Council, they were willing with their boldness to proclaim that Jesus is God. They spoke to the Jewish council and said you can do to us whatever you want to do, but all we know is what we have seen and heard. We cannot deny what we have witnessed.

Then Paul said in 2 Timothy 1:7: "For God hath not given us the spirit of fear; but of power, and of love, and of a sound mind." As a believer, you are able to stand before any man or magistrate and profess that you have authority in the name of Jesus. You can resist the devil in the name of Jesus because of the redemptive work of Christ.

Fifth, you are qualified to have authority because of your total dependence upon the Holy Spirit. If you step outside of the power of the Holy Spirit, you lose, but if you are led by the Spirit and depend upon Him, you can win. Those who walk not after the flesh, but walk after the Spirit, can begin today to walk in total victory and dominion in their lives. Jesus came that you might have life and have it more abundantly.

John said in 1 John 5:3: "Greater is He, that is in you, than He who is in the world." The preaching of the Church has been cross-centered when it should be also throne-centered. The cross is a place of defeat and victory, but the resurrection is a place of triumph and victory—healing, deliverance, restoration, and dominion.

The Church has authority on this earth through Christ. The source of that authority is Christ sitting at the right hand of the Father. When you were born again, you were raised to sit at the right hand of the Father. God gave you the authority to be called the sons of God. You are a partaker of the authority of Christ because you are reigning with Him.

When your faith is exercised, you have spiritual authority. Your faith does not rest on anything other than the Word of God. The Word of God says that you should not be moved by what you see or what you feel. You believe the Word when it says your assignment is to enforce the victory that Christ has won over Satan.

When your faith is exercised, you have spiritual authority. Your faith does not rest on anything other than the Word of God.

The devil cannot be a part of your life. Unless you give him permission to do so. Satan is the god of this world. He is running this world system. Men are blinded because they cannot see. Believers are in this world, but you are not of this world. Satan is not running you. God's plan for the world is that you rule and reign in life as kings and to rule over your circumstances.

According to 2 Corinthians 5:18, "Did you know that you are an ambassador for Christ?" An ambassador is someone who is from another country, but he is there on official government business. You are ambassadors for Christ. You are here to help reconcile men and women back to God. You have the authority from heaven behind us to enforce the victory.

Paul said that you must put on the whole armor of God and you will be ready for every situation that comes—with the helmet of salvation, the sword of the Spirit, the shield of faith. Are you ready for war? Are you ready to enforce the victory? You are seated in authority. "For above all principalities and powers and everything is subject to you."

You must begin to live in victory and power because you are seated in authority!

STUDY QUESTIONS

1. What did seating arrangements in the ancient world mean?
2. What does sitting at the right hand of God symbolize?
3. What five reasons does the author say that believers are qualified for authority?
4. Why does the author say preaching must also be throne-centered rather than cross-centered?

Chapter Seven

UNMASKING SATANIC LIES

SATAN'S BEST AND MOST EFFECTIVE STRATEGY IS TO convince you that he does not exist. Satan exists as the leader of the host of fallen angels. Jesus spoke of the devil and his angels, identifying them together. The Scriptures give the titles, origin, and works of Satan and his cohorts. From the beginning of time, Satan has been in defiance of God, and his mission is to destroy everything God created. Because Satan knows that his time is short (Revelation 12:12).

As a believer, it is vital that you realize that Satan is a personal, corruptive, and evil influence who manipu-lates and controls the world system.

As a believer, it is vital that you realize that Satan is a personal, corruptive, and evil influence who manipulates and controls the world system. There is a battle taking place between good and evil. Peter warned in 1 Peter 5:8 that "the devil is like a roaring lion, seeking those who he may devour." Satan is your number one enemy. He is not interested in your victory but in your destruction.

In John 10:10, Jesus said, "I came that you might have life, and have it more abundantly, but the thief comes to steal, kill, and destroy." Satan, from the very of beginning, according to Ezekiel 28:15, was given the title as Lucifer, son of the morning star, which is symbolic that he was the highest of angelic creatures.

The Scriptures say that Satan led a revolt in heaven against God to wrest power from Him. Satan and his angelic host were cast down from heaven (Revelation 12:7-12). Isaiah 14:12-15 describes the pride of Satan: "I will ascend to the heaven. I will exalt my throne above the stars of God. I will sit upon the mountain of the congregation. I will stand upon the heights of the clouds. I will be like the most high God." Hell was not created for man but for the devil and his angels. So if one ends up going to hell, it is not because God ever intended for him to go there. He went there because of his own decision.

TITLES OF SATAN

The word "Satan" means "adversary." He is the arch-enemy. From 1920 to 1933—the days of Prohibition—Al Capone was public enemy number one. But I submit that public enemy number one is the devil. If you, as a believer, can understand how he works, you will be victorious in resisting the devil when he comes to attack you.

DEVIL

Not only is Satan called the "adversary," but he is called the "devil." The word "devil" (diabolos) means "one who slanders." He goes before the throne of God and slanders you to God saying you are not worthy because you are a sinner. The devil tries his very best to undermine you.

In the first chapter of the Book of Job, Satan was walking to and fro upon the earth, and he came before God. God says to him, "Where have you come from?"

Satan replies, "I've been roaming to and fro upon the earth."

Then the Lord says to Satan, "Have you considered my servant Job?"

The devil says, "Yes, I've considered your servant Job. If you take the hedge from around him, if you take everything that you blessed him with, if you take it all from him, he'll curse you and he'll deny you."

God says, "I will permit you to remove the hedge from around him. I will allow you to take everything that he has. The one thing that you cannot take is his life." And so the devil took all Job's material possessions, including Job's children, But Job remained steadfast to God.

The devil came back to God and said, "If you allow me to strike his body and put disease on him, he will deny you."

What happens in your misery when you are to go through a difficult time in your life? Job's best friends showed up and said to him, "Job, the reason why you are in this mess is because there is sin in your life." But this was not true. They did not know that behind the scene God had permitted the devil to attack Job.

Sometimes when you are going through trials and tribulations in your life, it is not because you have sin in your life—it may be testing time. James 1:3 says: "Count all joy my brethren, when you fall into various trials, knowing that the testing of your faith produces steadfastness." Because you are going through a time of trial and difficulties does not mean that God has forsaken you. It does not mean there is sin in your life. It may mean that God is allowing the devil to sift you as wheat.

In Luke 22:31-34, the Lord told Peter, "Peter, I know you said you wouldn't deny me three times, but you will. The devil desires to have you and sift you like wheat. But when you are converted, strengthen your brethren." The best person who can strengthen you and develop you is a another believer who has gone through a similar experience.

Job was a righteous man. Job did not know that the providence of God was at work in his life. He thought God had abandoned him. God can allow things to happen in your life. It does not mean that He has taken His hand off your life. When you are going through difficult economic times, depression, and sickness in your life, you feel that God has abandoned you. No!

You must always know that God is ever present. Even Jesus felt like that. When He was on the cross, He cried out, "My God, my God, why has Thou forsaken me?" (Matthew 27:46). He felt abandoned. He felt all alone.

BEELZEBUB

The word "Beelzebub" means the "prince of evil." There is a hierarchical structure that exists within the demonic world. Satan is on top and his emissaries are at work on his behalf all over the world. (He is also called "Baal"—the low one. He is referred to in Genesis 3:5 and Revelation 12:9 as the "old serpent." He was in the Garden of Eden.)

THE GOD OF THIS WORLD

2 Corinthians 4:4 describes Satan as the "god of this world." This is his territory—his domain. He is called the "prince of this world" in John 12:31. In Ephesians 2:2, he is called the "prince of the power of the air." In Revelation 20:2, he is called a "dragon." 2 Corinthians 11:14 says that he is able to change himself, such as masquerading himself into an angel of light.

THE FATHER OF LIES

In John 8:44, Satan is called the "father of lies." That is his nature: to deceive and to be deceptive. Satan is so clever that people believe what they are doing is right when in fact it is wrong (2 Thessalonians 2:13-14).

SATAN'S LIMITATIONS

SATAN IS NOT OMNIPOTENT

Satan, the diabolical creature, is limited in his strategy to defeat you. First, he is not omnipotent, that is, he is not all powerful. Satan is limited in his power by God. Satan cannot force people to obey him. As an excuse, many use the phrase "the devil made me do it." But this is not correct. The devil did not make you "do it." You did it because we wanted to. The devil never gives us what you do not want. He always gives you what you want. When you understand his power, then he cannot force you to obey him. He can tempt you and entice you, but he has no power to force you to transgress God's will.

In Matthew 4:1ff, Jesus was led by the Spirit into the wilderness to be tempted by the devil. The devil said to Jesus, "Are you hungry?" He knew Jesus was hungry because He had been in the wilderness for 40 days. Satan will not tempt you with desires you do not have, but the desires you really have. Satan said, "If you're the Son of God. That's who you say you are. And you are here hungry. Turn these stones into bread."

And Jesus quoted from Deuteronomy 8:12, "Man shall not live by bread alone, but every word that proceeds out of the mouth of God." The devil then took Him to the pinnacle of the temple and said, "If you're the son of God, why don't you jump off from here and show the people how spectacular and the marvelous feats you can do."

Again, quoting from the Scriptures, Jesus said, "You shall not tempt the Lord, thy God."

Then the devil said, "Jesus, you don't have to go to the cross and die. If you want the masses of people to follow you, fall down and worship me, and I will give you all the kingdoms of this world."

And Jesus said, "You shall only worship the Lord, thy God."

The only way Jesus was ever able to defeat the devil was by using the Scriptures. If you do not know the Scriptures, then you cannot defeat the devil. The devil knows the Scriptures better than you do. In reading Genesis 3:11ff, he changed one word that God said. God said, "Every tree in the garden, thou shall freely eat, but the tree of good and evil that is in the middle of the garden thou shall not eat, for on the day you eat you will surely die."

Satan said, "You will *not* surely die. You're going to become just like God, knowing good and evil." And that's exactly what they did. They trusted the devil rather than trusting what God had said.

SATAN IS NOT OMNISCIENT

Satan is clever but he is not all-knowing. He knows how to attack, hurt, and destroy. That is why the Scriptures refers to him as a roaring lion, going around seeking those whom he may devour. He does not know all things, but he knows how to tempt you. 1 John 2:16 says: "Love not the world neither the things in the world for they are the lust of the flesh, the lust of the eyes, and the pride of life." In James 1:13, James said, "Let no man say he is tempted of God for God tempts no man. Each man is tempted when he is lured away by his own lust. When lust is fully conceived, it brings forth sin, and sin brings forth death."

SATAN IS NOT OMNIPRESENT

Satan is not omnipresent; he cannot be everywhere at the same time. He cannot be in more than one place at a time.

When he was with Jesus, he was nowhere else. When he left Jesus, it was recorded. Since Satan cannot be everywhere, he has demons who are dispatched at his pleasure. He has a kingdom of his own. Jesus, in Matthew 12:26, spoke of this satanic kingdom.

The devil also works through humans to accomplish his work. He did it with Judas. "Satan entered the heart of Judas" (John 13:2). We even have seen people lie for no reason at all. Satan will use the mouths of people to do his bidding (Acts 5:1-11). In Acts 8:9-11, Phillip went down to the city of Samaria and preached the gospel. The entire city of Samaria was converted to Christ. But there was also a man in Samaria named Simon the sorcerer. Phillip converted him to Christ, but Simon deceived the people with all types of magic.

ACTIVITIES OF SATAN DENOTE HIS POWER

Luke 8:26-39 tells of a man who lived out in the tombs. When Jesus met the man, he asked, "What is your name?"

The man responded, "My name is Legion." There were so many demons inside of him that he did not know who he was and Jesus cast out the demons in the man.

Those of us who live in Western Civilization believe that because of technology, science, and education, there is no reason to believe in the supernatural or to be superstitious. But why is it that such a large percentage of the world's population believes in demonic creatures or demonic spirits? We are in a warfare between the Kingdom of God and the kingdom of Satan. Which side are you on?

HOW TO IDENTIFY A SATANIC ATTACK

When criticism and accusations are made against you, you must determine whether these are from God or a satanic attack.

When criticism and accusations are made against you, you must determine whether these are from God or a satanic attack. Do these spoken words come from a healthy, strong, polite relationship? Is this person someone you can trust?

Were these words of correction spoken out of love or out of anger because the Scriptures tell us to speak the truth in of love (Ephesians 4:15). Were these words intended to improve and build you up? Does the person who spoke these words have God's direction to teach you? You must ask yourself, have I violated any specific biblical principles? Were the words the person was using to correct or tear you down? Are they accusing words? Did the words attempt to hinder what is good? Are the words spoken from hate? Do the words attempt to obstruct you from doing what God has called you to do? Are the words spoken in false accusation about your motives or purposes?

Why do I raise these questions? In Matthew 16:21ff, Jesus spoke to Peter saying "Flesh and blood has not revealed this to you but my Father which is in heaven." Peter had just declared, "Thou art the Christ, the Son of the living God."

When Jesus told His disciples that He was going to Jerusalem to die, Peter said, "No, not so, Lord."

Jesus then said to Peter, "Get behind me, Satan, for your mind is not on the things of God but on the things of the devil." You can speak the Word of God one moment, and then the next moment the devil can enter your heart and dictate what you may be thinking or speaking, which will be contrary to the Word of God.

POSSESSION VERSUS INFLUENCE

When it comes to believers, demonic spirits cannot possess you, but they certainly can influence you. But the unbeliever can be under demonic possession. 1 Timothy 4:1 says: "The Spirit speaks expressly that in the latter time, some shall depart from the faith." How will they depart Paul? Paul said, by giving heed to seducing spirits, they seduce people with counterfeit teaching which is adverse to God's will..

Demons maintain conflict with believers who are spiritual (Ephesians 6:12). And all unbelievers are open to demonic possession. In Ephesians 2:2, Paul said that "we were dead in our trespass and sins." He continued, "By nature they are the children of wrath." They lived according to the prince of this world.

The believers' resources for dealing with demonic spirits are prayer, fasting, and the Scriptures.

The believers' resources for dealing with demonic spirits are prayer, fasting, and the Scriptures (Matthew 17:21). You must put on the whole armor of God (Ephesians 6:14-18). How are we going to fight against the devil if you do not have your weapons of war? You have to gird your feet with the gospel of peace and get ready for war.

TEST FOR DEALING WITH DEMONS

There are four tests to determine whether you are dealing with a demon if you are sick or diseased.

First, demons always appear—for the most part, in the dark. Second, demons deny the personality of Satan. Third, demons hate the name of the Lord Jesus. Fourth, demons always cast contempt on the inspiration of the Scriptures.

Acts 10:38 says: Jesus went about doing good to all those who were oppressed by the devil. The devil does not want you to see the truth. If you follow these four tests, you can determine whether you are dealing with a demon.

HOW TO OVERCOME THE DEVIL

James 4:6: "God gives more grace wherefore he said God resisted the proud, giving grace unto the humble." If you can resist the devil, he will flee from you. You can overcome the devil if you learn his methods, schemes, and strategy. You can live like God intended for you to live. You can win because John said "greater is He that is in you, than he that is in the world."

STUDY QUESTIONS

1. What is Satan's most effective strategy?
2. What are the titles associated with Satan?
3. Jesus defined Satan's threefold strategy in John 10:10. What is it?
4. Why is Satan called the "god of this world"?
5. What are the three specific ways the author mentions that Satan is limited?
6. What is the believer's key arsenal or weapon in defeating Satan?

7. What does the author recommend in identifying a Satanic attack?
8. What is the difference between possession and influence?
9. What are the four specific ways the author mentions for dealing with demons?
10. How does Satan relate to the demonic kingdom?

Chapter Eight

DECLARE WAR ON THE DEVIL

As I previously mentioned, you are in a war and you are under spiritual attack. Because you are in a spiritual battle, you must put on the whole armor of God. God declared war on Satan. Revelation 12: 7-9 says there was a war in heaven between the archangel Michael and Lucifer, who was cast down to Earth. God rules by His sovereign power.

Paul, in 2 Corinthians 4:1ff, said that Satan is the god of this world. He deceived Adam and Eve by telling them they would become just like God in knowing good from evil. As a result of their disobedience, sin and death came into the world. You need to know who you are if you are going to be victorious over him.

In 2 Corinthians 4:1, Paul said, "The god of this world blinds the minds of them which believe not, lest the light of the glorious gospel of Christ, who is the image of God, should shine unto them." When your life is directed by Satan, then you are under his power. In Ephesians 2:1, Paul said, "Wherein in time past you walked according to the course of this world, according to the prince of the power of the air, the spirit that now works in the children of disobedience." God said that we once lived according to the pattern of this world, and according to the power of Satan. There is a satanic spirit at work in the sons of disobedience.

Satan uses deception to control your mind. His desire is to keep you from seeing the truth. Jesus said in John 8:44-45, "You are of your father the devil, and the lusts of your father you will do. He was a murderer from the beginning, and abode not in the truth, because there is no truth in him. When he speaks a lie, he speaks of his own: for he is a liar, and the father of it. And because I tell you the truth, you believe me not."

Peter warned in 1 Peter 5:8: "Be sober, be vigilant; because your adversary the devil, as a roaring lion, walks about, seeking whom he may devour." The devil goes around and intimidates believers. Simply put, he is a big bully, but if you understand that he is a big bully and you decide that you will fight back, he will run. What he is depending on is psyching you out. One of the greatest athletes was heavyweight boxing champion Muhammad Ali. Ali had the ability to psyche out an opponent, to make an opponent think that he was already beaten. Satan wants you to think that you are already defeated.

Paul says in Ephesians 6:11: "Put on the whole armor of God, that you may be able to stand against the wiles of the devil." The word "wiles" or "scheme" means "methods." Satan has a strategy and once you understand what his strategy is to defeat you, then you are in a position to be able to overcome whatever the devil throws at you.

Satan has a strategy and once you understand what his strategy is to defeat you, then you are in a position to be able to overcome whatever the devil throws at you.

WHO YOU ARE IN CHRIST

As you realize who you are in Christ, you will be able to effectively win the battle. In Ephesians 1:17, Paul said, "That the God of our Lord Jesus Christ, the Father of glory, may give unto you the spirit of wisdom and revelation in the knowledge of him." God will give you a spirit of wisdom. Wisdom is the skillful use of God's knowledge applied in your life. As we follow God's will, He will provide directives.

God's word's will always lead to predictable results.

God's word's will always lead to predictable results. If you lack wisdom, you must ask God for He gives to all liberally, but you need to ask in faith. Paul said, "And what is the exceeding greatness of His power to us who believe, according to the working of His mighty power." That same power God used to raise Christ from the dead is the same power that He has made available to the believer. God makes the same power available to you. "Which He wrought in Christ, when He raised Him from the dead, and set Him at His own right hand in the heavenly places, Far above all principality, and power, and might, and dominion, and every name that is named, not only in this world, but also in that which is to come."

To put it simply, God raised Jesus from the dead, but He also raised Him and sat Him at His right hand. The right hand represents God's power, and Jesus is sitting at the right hand of God's power, ruling over every power, potentate, and principality. And His name is above every name, that of the name of Jesus. Every knee shall bow and every tongue shall confess that Jesus is Lord.

YOU HAVE POWER

In Ephesians 2:5, Paul said that "God has made us alive together with Christ [by grace we are saved]. And hath raised us up together, and made us sit together in heavenly places in Christ Jesus; that in the ages to come He might show the exceeding riches of his grace in His kindness toward us through Christ Jesus."

Jesus said in Matthew 28:18-20: "All power in heaven and on earth has been given unto me." Jesus is sitting on the right hand of the Father. As a believer, you are also sitting on the right hand of the Father with Christ. And if we are sitting with Jesus, you have power. What does Jesus have power over? He has power over all the demons, death, and sin.

Do not let anyone convince you that you do not have any power. God has delegated you with power. As an example, New York City gives every policeman, whether he is fresh out of the academy or has been on the force for 30 years, power to do his job. He has been given that power representatively in the badge he wears and the gun he carries. When he steps into the traffic, he has the power to stop traffic. Now, physically, he is just like you, but his power does not come from himself. His power comes from the city of New York.

So whatever the policeman says, if it is in accordance with the law, you are bound and obligated to obey. Jesus said in John 1:12-13: "But as many as received him, to them gave He power to become the sons of God, even to them that believe on His name: Which were born, not of blood, nor of the will of the flesh, nor of the will of man, but of God." If you are a child of God, God has designated you with authority to do business in His name. All you have to do is exercise the power that has been given to you.

If you are a child of God, God has designated you with authority to do business in His name. All you have to do is exercise the power that has been given to you.

The devil wants to deceive you and convince you that you do not have any power. Hebrews 2:14: "Forasmuch then as the children are partakers of flesh and blood, he also himself likewise took part of the same; that through death he might destroy him that had the power of death, that is, the devil."

In 1 Peter 5:9, Peter said, "Casting all your care upon him; for he cares for you." Do you have any cares? Anxiety?

Stress? Peter said, "Cast all of your cares upon Him, for he cares about you. Be sober, be vigilant; because your adversary, the devil, as a roaring lion, walks about, seeking whom he may devour; who resist steadfast in the faith, knowing that the same afflictions are accomplished in your brethren that are in the world." Why would Peter tell you to resist him if you could not resist him or if you did not have power.

The purpose in attending church and reading your Bible is to be strong. You cannot be victorious as a Christian, isolated from the church. The church must be a priority in your life. You cannot rearrange your schedule for somebody else to keep you from coming to church. If you tell others that you are going to church and they can come with you. Until we get real about God, God is not going to be real about you.

You have to quit "playing church," that is, you have to quit playing part-time Christianity. This will not get you anywhere. You must be serious about God. You go to church, pray, and have fellowship with other Christians. Right beliefs produce right behavior which produces right results, and when you resist the devil, he will flee. "But the God of all grace, who hath called us unto his eternal glory by Christ Jesus, after that ye have suffered a while, make you perfect, establish, strengthen, and settle you." You need to make God first in our lives.

1 John 3:8 says: "He that commits sin is of the devil; for

the devil sinned from the beginning." There is no middle ground—either you are serving the devil or you are serving Christ. "For this purpose the Son of God was manifested, that He might destroy the works of the devil." He has already been defeated. What you have to do is enforce the victory, but the victory begins first with you.

If you are in Christ, Satan has no dominion in your life.

If you are in Christ, Satan has no dominion in your life. The devil watches your behavior. He has been studying you for a long time. He does not know what you are going to do. He cannot read your mind, but he watches you. Based on your past performance, he knows what you like. He sets you up for a fall!

Paul said in 2 Corinthians 10:3-5 that the devil places a thought into your mind. A temptation is a legitimate need you have—but you choose to let Satan meet that need rather than God. Satan puts a thought into your mind by suggestion and you sit there and meditate on that thought. You think about how you can do this without getting caught. Satan is never going to tempt you with something that you do not want, especially when it makes you feel good and brings you pleasure.

In 1 John 2:15, John said, "Love not the world, nor the things in the world, for they are the lust of flesh." It feels good to our flesh. The music you listen to can be seductive. You have to be careful about what you see and what you listen to. You get caught up in the moment. You cannot listen to seductive music. What is the music telling us? Your mind is programmed by what you listen to. You must put on the whole armor of God.

WEAPONS IN THE ARMOR OF GOD

These weapons are for defense. In other words, you have to put these on for protection.

BELT OF TRUTH

If you are going to defeat the devil, you have to learn to live by the truth. What is the truth? The truth is the Word of God. Jesus said, "If you continue in my word, then truly you are my disciple indeed and you shall know the truth and the truth shall set you free" (John 8:32-33).

BREASTPLATE OF RIGHTEOUSNESS

What does it mean to be the righteousness of God? The word "righteousness" means "to be declared innocent." Standing before the judge in court, you do not know what type of sentence the judge is going to hand down. You are just standing there before the mercy of the court. Then the judge says, "Your crime and your punishment have already been taken care of. You're innocent. You can go." That is the meaning of being righteous. It means to stand before God guiltless.

Romans 8:1 says: "There is no condemnation for those of us who are in Christ." If you are in Christ, no one has the right to condemn you because nobody has the power to save or condemn. They do not have power to put anyone in heaven or in hell. If you really know the truth about the matter, you are to be so glad about your situation that you do not have time to be worried about anyone else's situation.

SHOES OF PEACE

Peace is not about the absence of strife and conflict, but it means nothing is broken and nothing is lacking! When the Jews talked about having peace, they talked about both God's material blessings, as well as God's spiritual blessings. Since your feet are supposed to be peace, you must not create havoc; you want to create peace.

SHIELD OF FAITH

Your faith is absolutely essential to spiritual warfare. If you loose our faith, you have lost the battle. Your faith is to be the shield to protect you and to tell you to keep going when everyone else is telling you to stop. When discouragement comes, your faith tells you that you do not have time to get depressed.

HELMET OF SALVATION

You must know without a shadow of a doubt that you are saved! We are saved not because of what you have done but because of what Jesus has done. Salvation means that God not only saved you but he rescued you.

SWORD OF THE SPIRIT

Last of all, the only offensive weapon you have in the war is the sword of the Spirit. You have to know the Bible. The spoken word is never separated from the revealed and written word. We have to master the written word to the point that when you go into battle, you can speak the Word of God!

STUDY QUESTIONS

1. Why does the author say it is important for believers to know who they are in Christ?
2. What kind of power or authority does the believer possess?
3. Why is the believer spiritual armor so important in spiritual warfare?
4. What are the six essential pieces of armor of the soldier for battle?

OTHER BOOKS BY DR. KENNETH GILMORE

Leadership In African American Churches of Christ

The New Covenant: Your Rights and Privileges

What Is Biblical Faith?

The Battle for the Mind

Bring Me The Book

The Apostle's Doctrine

Money: God's Financial Plan For Your Life

Unmasking Satanic Lies

The Authority of The Believer

Principle Centered Living

The Power of The Tongue

Prayer, The Key To Success

God's Spiritual Laws

What Kind of Man Are You

How To Have Success With God

The Decision Is In Your Hand

Bring Me the Book

Set for the Defense

TAPE SERIES BY DR. KENNETH GILMORE

New Covenant: Your Rights	2 Tapes
What Is Biblical Faith?	2 Tapes
How To Have Success With God	5 Tapes
Money: God's Financial Plan	2 Tapes
Unmasking Satanic Lies	2 Tapes
The Authority of The Believer	4 Tapes

The Power of The Tongue	3 Tapes
God's Spiritual Laws	6 Tapes
What Kind of Man Are You?	3 Tapes
Principle Centered Living	3 Tapes
The New Testament Church, Which One Is True?	2 Tapes
The Battle For The Mind	4 Tapes
Prayer	4 Tapes

BECOME A COVENANT TRUTH PARTNER WITH KENNETH GILMORE MINISTRIES!

Because of the power that comes through fellowship, commitment and partnership, we invite you to join with Dr. Kenneth Gilmore in fulfilling the vision God has given him. Dr. Gilmore has been given a mandate to teach the Word of God in simple terms so that all can understand.

It's easy to become a Covenant Truth Partner. Simply fill out the form on page 101 and mail it to:

Kenneth Gilmore Ministries
150 S.E. 74th Street
Gainesville, Florida 32641

phone: 352-376-8843
email: Kgmin@bellsouth .net

Our prayer for you is that as you enter covenant with us, God's blessings and manifold riches will be unleashed in your life.

Covenant Truth Partners have sought the Lord and received His confirmation of the worth of this ministry. Therefore, Partners are more than friends, they are loyal, trusted allies in the ministry. We value all of our Covenant Truth Partners and hold them up to God in prayer, minister to them with a personal monthly letter and offer from time to time discounted products for spiritual edification and growth.

THERE IS VALUE IN COVENANT TRUTH PARTNERSHIP!

Yes. I'd like to become a Covenant Truth Partner in prayer and financial support with Kenneth Gilmore Ministries.

____

Last Name

____

First Name Middle Initial

____

Street Address Apartment #

____

City State Zip

You can count on me for a monthly pledge of:

❑ $1,000 ❑ $500 ❑ $100

❑ $50 ❑ $25 ❑ $______

❑ One time gift of $____________

www.ingramcontent.com/pod-product-compliance
Lightning Source LLC
LaVergne TN
LVHW050537100826
845148LV00002B/596

* 9 7 8 0 9 7 4 8 9 4 4 5 4 *